WORLD
DOMINION

All Scripture quotations are from the King James Version of the Holy Bible.

Printed in the United States of America

ISBN 1-57558-078-0

WORLD DOMINION

FROM THE
TOWER OF BABEL
TO THE
MARK OF THE BEAST

Vaughn Shatzer

Table of Contents

Part I

From the Tower of Babel to the Mark of the Beast

Chapter 1

The New World Disorder

Revelation 13 is one of the most awesome chapters in the Word of God. It takes place during the middle of the seven-year Tribulation period, according to verse five. It gives a graphic description of two satanic and demon-possessed men, who are both called beasts.

We know these two beasts are literal men because they are both cast into the lake of fire. Revelation 19:20 states:

> And the beast was taken, and with him the false prophet that wrought miracles before him, with which he deceived them that had received the mark of the beast, and them that worshipped his image. These both were cast alive into a lake of fire burning with brimstone.

We also know that the first beast, who Christians have referred to as Antichrist, will kill the two witnesses, after they have prophesied for three and one-half years (Rev. 11:3–7).

The next graphic description given in Revelation 13 describes four world systems which will be run and ruled by the first beast, Antichrist. These four world systems include a world government, a world military, a world religion, and a world economy.

Amazingly, these four world systems are coming together at breathtaking speed right before our very eyes. These world systems have a name with which we are familiar, "The New World Order," which promises to usher in an era of peace, prosperity, justice, and harmony.[1] Sadly, this is another lie from the father of lies, the Devil (John 8:44).

In reality, the New World Order will ultimately usher in the most horrible form of totalitarian government the world has ever known.

This diabolical global agenda, conjured up by Satan himself, will enslave the earth's inhabitants. There will be virtually no place to hide from the World Police, the new super computers, and global positioning satellites. If you think it's bad now, wait until the restraining power of the Holy Spirit is removed and he is taken out of the way (2 Thess. 2:6–7). At the same exact moment, "in the twinkling of an eye . . . the dead in Christ shall rise first: Then we which are alive and remain shall be caught up together with them in the clouds, to meet the Lord in the air: and so shall we ever be with the Lord" (1 Cor. 15:52; 1 Thess. 4:16–17). All true Christians will be gone and everyone else will be left behind to endure earth's darkest hour. Then, according to Second Thessalonians 2:3–8, the "man of sin," the "son of perdition," the "Wicked" one, the Antichrist will be revealed. What we are seeing right now is a Sunday school picnic compared to the dictatorial reign of Antichrist, who will be in charge of the New World Order during the horrendous Tribulation period.

There is good news. First, God is in complete control of everything that happens, including all the details in the book of Revelation. Second, according to Revelation 19, Jesus Christ will return with armies of ten thousands of his saints, at the end of the seven-year Tribulation period. He will defeat the Antichrist and his world military at the Battle of Armageddon. Jesus Christ, the "King of Kings and Lord of Lords," will then set up His everlasting kingdom (Dan. 7:14, 27). This will begin His thousand-year reign on earth (Rev. 20:4). Praise the Lord!

Now that we have an overview of Revelation 13 and know the final victory will be won with the return of Christ, let's discuss and document some details of the New World Order. Most of us became familiar with the phrase "New World Order" in the eighties. The New World Order is really not new. Its beginning goes back thousands of years to the Tower of Babel, described in Genesis 10–11. This is when Nimrod "began to be a mighty one in the earth . . . and the beginning of his kingdom was Babel." The literal Hebrew definition for these words means, "the first powerful tyrant to unify by

TAB. LXXIII.

GENESIS Cap. XI. v. 4.
Scenographia Turris.

I. Buch Mosis Cap. XI. v. 4.
Der Perspectivische Riß des Thurns

force and become famous." In addition, all the people were of one language, one speech, and said, "Let us make us a name." This first attempt of the New World Order failed because of God's divine intervention. Since that time, many attempts have been made but also ended in failure. Today, in the new millennium, the New World Order is alive and well, as we shall soon find out.

Even the FBI has a thirty-two–page report entitled "Project Megiddo" (Document A). It contains a section about the "New World Order Conspiracy Theory." Some of the warnings found in "Project Megiddo" are timely and well taken, but the report paints all Christians as "extremists." The report defines an extremist as one who believes in the end of the world and the Second Coming of Christ.

Our former president, George Bush, used the phrase "New World Order" over two hundred times[2] during his administration. President Bush defined the details of the New World Order in a speech at the National Religious Broadcasters Convention in Washington, D.C. To an audience of about four thousand people, he implied: "You know what is going to solve all our problems? There is something called

President Bush addresses a joint session of Congress at the end of the war with Iraq.

President George Bush at the National Religious Broadcasters convention.

the New World Order. When this comes in, it's going to bring peace as we have never seen. We are going to be able to lay down all our weapons. The New World Order is the solution to all our problems."[3]

If only President Bush had known! The peace of the New World Order will be a false peace and a living nightmare come true. First Thessalonians 5:3 states: "For when they shall say, Peace and safety; then sudden destruction cometh upon them, as travail upon a woman with child; and they shall not escape."

By the mid-nineties, hundreds of world leaders and thousands of businessmen would unite in San Francisco, California, to promote the New World Order. Who do you think was heading up this big meeting? An article, dated February 3, 1995, from one of California's largest newspapers, the *San Francisco Chronicle,* states:

Former Soviet President Mikhail Gorbachev has asked hundreds of world leaders and thousands of business people to join him in

Gorbachev to Convene Meeting in S.F. in Fall

Invitees include Bush, Thatcher, Tutu

By Edward Epstein
Chronicle Staff Writer

Former Soviet President Mikhail Gorbachev has asked hundreds of world leaders and thousands of business people to join him in San Francisco next autumn to discuss the state of the world.

The Gorbachev Foundation U.S.A., based in the Presidio, has already lined up an array of co-chairmen for the five-day conference, which will be held at the Fairmont Hotel. They include former President George Bush, former Prime Minister Margaret Thatcher of Britain, President Vaclav Havel of the Czech Republic, Nobel Peace Prize winners Archbishop Desmond Tutu and Rigoberta Menchu, cable TV magnate Ted Turner and former Japanese Prime Minister Yasuhiro Nakasone.

The idea behind the forum, from September 27 to October 1, is to "convene a conversation to look at fundamental priorities and values that the world should embrace as it moves beyond the Cold War," said Jim Garrison, the foundation's president.

Hopes for a new world order after the end of the Cold War have dimmed. "There appears to be a great cynicism everywhere with government," said former Senator Alan Cranston, D-Calif., chairman of the Gorbachev Foundation USA. "And there is a yearning for new directions,"

Organizers have also invited hundreds of participants from many walks of life either to address the conference or to participate in 20 smaller round tables that will examine everything from the future of the nation state to the problems of crime, pollution, new technologies and the rights of businesses and individuals.

Others who have been invited include Vice President Al Gore, President Nelson Mandela of South Africa, ABC News' Ted Koppel, novelist Isabel Allende, Microsoft chairman William Gates, Mother Teresa, explorer Thor Heyerdahl, Body Shop founder Anita Roddick and futurist Alvin Toffler. Some have accepted, but it is too early to know whether all will attend.

About 8,000 business leaders from 75 countries are being invited to attend as paying participants, at $5,000 a person.

Garrison said Gorbachev wants the exchange of ideas to lead to creation of an informal brain trust that will meet during the next several years. Projects that might be undertaken include a so-called Earth Charter, described as an environmental bill of rights, and an attempt to eliminate all nuclear weapons by the year 2010.

San Francisco next autumn to discuss the state of the world. The idea behind the forum, from September 27 to October 1, is to . . . look at fundamental priorities and values that the world should embrace. Hopes for a new world order . . . have dimmed, "and there is a yearning for new directions" said former Senator Alan Cranston, D-California, chairman of the Gorbachev Foundation, U.S.A.

Amazingly, Mikhail Gorbachev has been holding "State of the World Forums" in our own backyard since 1995. Remember now, "the idea behind the forum is to look at fundamental priorities and values which the world should embrace." There was a list of forty-two presentations recorded at the 1995 Forum.[4] You will be shocked at the similarities between the sugarcoated titles and the four world systems of Revelation 13: "Emerging Global Political and Security Trends," "Global Security," "Seeking Genuine Disarmament," "The Global Crisis of Spirit and the Search for Meaning," "The New Science of the Sacred," and "Technology and Labor in the Global Economy." The other thirty-eight presentations revolve around the same basic themes.

The State of the World Forum included an array of cochairmen, namely former president George Bush, former British prime minister Margaret Thatcher, Nobel Peace Prize winner Archbishop Desmond Tutu, and cable TV magnate Ted Turner. The Forum was also a "coming-out party" for New Age elitists. Among those present were John Denver, Shirley MacLaine, Carl Sagan, Barbara Marx Hubbard, Maurice Strong, Robert Muller, and Michael Murphy, just to name a few. The annual "State of the Forum" meetings are being held by the Gorbachev Foundation U.S.A. at the Presidio in San Francisco. The Presidio, at one time, was one of America's most hallowed U.S. military bases, built to defend America. Now it is being used by Mikhail Gorbachev to promote the blueprint for the New World Order — a global *perestroika* — right in our own backyard. How sad! For more information on the "State of the World

Forums," access their website at *www.worldforum.org.*

Finally, this article from the *San Francisco Chronicle* stated that Mikhail Gorbachev wanted to create an "informal brain trust," for a so-called "Earth Charter,"[5] described as an "environmental bill of rights." Both the "informal brain trust" and "Earth Charter" are now realities through his special, powerful, and international organization, "Green Cross Family."[6] Gorbachev's website for "Green Cross Family" opens with the following words: "We need a new system of values, a system of the organic unity between mankind and nature and the ethic of global responsibility." This statement has become Gorbachev's campaign slogan. This radical, all-encompassing, planetary document called "The Earth Charter" is a bill of rights for the planet. If implemented, it would give the environment far greater rights than "we the people." Humanity would literally become a slave to the earth and to the global regime who would enforce these mandates.

Gorbachev described his new "Earth Charter" as "a new set of rules to guide humanity."[7] He also stated: "My hope is that this charter will be a kind of Ten Commandments, a Sermon on the Mount, that provides a guide for human behavior toward the environment, in the next century and beyond."[8]

As you read the opening paragraphs that form the preamble to the "Earth Charter" (Document B), it reminds you of the ancient pagan worship of Mother Earth, combined with the New Age movement. Here are a few of the "buzz" words: "interdependent world," "interconnected," "interrelated," "global interdependence," "world community," "global partnership," "global civilization," and "sustainable development."

The sixteen general principles, which consist of another forty-seven subprinciples, in the "Earth Charter" give the details of how to use the "Environmental Crisis" for world government. Another statement made by Gorbachev sums it all up in a neat package: "The environmental crisis is the cornerstone for the New World Order."[9]

The "Earth Charter" is to be presented to the General Assembly of the United Nations for ratification. They hoped to have it adopted in the year 2000.[10] For more information, read the "Earth Charter" for yourself at their website.

Chapter 2

World Government

Let's move on to the evidence and details of the four world systems which make up the New World Order. The first world system is world government. Revelation 13:7 states: ". . . and power was given him over all kindreds, and tongues, and nations." This person referred to in this passage is the first beast, the Wicked One or Antichrist, the world dictator. He will have power over all kindreds, which means races, including red, yellow, black, and white, all tongues, meaning every language, and all nations. The word "power" used here in verse seven and also verses four, five, and twelve, is an interesting word in the Greek language. It is the word *exooseeah,* which means "superhuman" or "magistrate." The word magistrate means "a public civil officer with the executive government." A king is the highest or first magistrate, as is the president of the United States. This verse could literally read "superhuman and highest governmental power was given to Antichrist to rule the world." We know Antichrist will have superhuman power because he is possessed by Satan himself.

Since the Antichrist will be in charge of the world government, he will need a world constitution. Guess what! There is already a world constitution drafted. In 1987 the World Constitution and Parliament Association (WCPA),[11] located in Lakewood, Colorado, drafted this fifty-page document entitled "A Constitution for the Federation of Earth."[12] The World Constitution and Parliament Association was founded back in 1959, and presently has over fifteen million members from more than eighty countries.[13] The membership consists of prime ministers, ambassadors, key members of the United Nations, dignitaries, influential financiers and attorneys, as well as leading educators and religious leaders. WCPA also boasts a net-work of more than four hundred thirty organizations worldwide.[14] In reality, the WCPA is a storefront for one-worlders, United Na-tions, New Age organizations, and even the World Council of Church-es.

Let's examine the World Constitution (see *Foundational Docu-ments of the New World Order*). One of the first statements: "Re-sponsible world government is at least forty-seven years overdue." There is also a "Partial List of World Problems," which the WCPA cites for needing a world government. Most of the "problems" deal with the environment, military disarmament, world hunger, and the economy. The World Constitution contains a preamble and nineteen articles. The preamble reads like a page out of a New Age occult manual. Here is a portion of it:

> Realizing that Humanity today has come to a turning point in his-tory and that we are on the threshold of a new world order which promises to usher in an era of peace, prosperity, justice, and har-mony. Conscious that humanity is one . . . and that the principles of unity in diversity is the basis for a new age. . . . Conscious of the inescapable reality that the greatest hope for the survival of life on earth is the establishment of a democratic world government we, citizens of the world, hereby resolve to establish a world feder-ation to be governed in accordance with this constitution for the federation of Earth.

Articles I through III of the World Constitution cover the broad func-tions, basic structure, and organs of the world government. They will regulate virtually every aspect of life, from communications and transportation to world trade and all other global processes.

Article IV will prohibit and eliminate the design, testing, manu-facture, sale, purchase, use, and possession of weapons of mass de-struction. It will also prohibit or regulate all lethal weapons, which the World Parliament may decide. This means there will be complete gun control and no more national defense. This article will also create a world financial banking and credit union, along with a World Economic Development Organization.

Amazingly, the first four articles of the World Constitution set up three out of the four world systems — a world government, a world military, and a world economy — which will be run and ruled by Antichrist.

Articles V and VI set up a world parliament and world executive. One of their functions would be to approve, amend, or reject international laws developed prior to the advent of world government. With a swipe of a pen, this article would do away with our God-given rights and our God-ordained U.S. Constitution and Bill of Rights.

Article VIII is the Integrative Complex. One of the seven agencies created under this branch is "The World Boundaries and Election Administration." It will be headed by a ten-member commission, in addition to the senior administrator from ten World Magna Regions. This sounds like the end-time scenario of the ten kings and Antichrist in Daniel 7:24: "And the ten horns out of this kingdom are ten kings that shall arise: and another shall rise after them. . . ." Verse twenty-five goes on to tell us that the one individual (Antichrist) who rules over the other ten kings and the whole earth will blaspheme God, persecute the saints, change laws, and will rule the world for "a time and times and the dividing of time," which is three and one-half years according to the original Aramaic words in verse twenty-five.

That is the bad news, but here is the good news. Daniel 7:26–27 tells us that in the end, God will judge and destroy the Antichrist's kingdom and set up an everlasting kingdom:

> But the judgment shall sit, and they shall take away his dominion, to consume and to destroy it unto the end. And the kingdom and dominion, and the greatness of the kingdom under the whole heaven, shall be given to the people of the saints of the most High,

whose kingdom is an everlasting kingdom, and all dominions shall serve and obey him.

If only the fifteen million members of the World Constitution and Parliament Association would read, heed, and accept the Word of God as truth, they could be a part of this everlasting kingdom. We need to pray for them.

Article IX sets up the World Judiciary, with a World Supreme Court and world judges, elected from the ten World Magna Regions.

Article X creates the "Enforcement System" that includes the "World Police." That's right! The World Police. Does that send chills down your spine? According to sections A and B, the "Enforcement System" functions will be investigation, apprehension, arrest, prosecution, remedies, correction, and conflict resolution. Section C describes the World Police who will be responsible for searches, apprehension, and arrest of individuals responsible for violations of world law. Section D describes the "Means of Enforcement," which includes denial of financial credit, revocation of licenses, impounding of equipment, imprisonment, or isolation and other means, appropriate to the specific situation.

This article reminds us of Revelation 13:17 where you will not be able to buy or sell, unless you have taken the mark of the beast (666). We will discuss the mark of the beast in great detail a little later.

Article XV, Section B, sets up a Primary World Capital. We know from Revelation 17–18 this world capital or city will be named Babylon. We also know this city or system will be destroyed in one hour.

Article XVII covers the ratification and implementation process of the "World Constitution for the Federation of Earth." Section D issues an invitation to a very powerful worldwide organization to transfer personnel, facilities, equipment, resources, and allegiance to the Federation of Earth and to the world government thereof. Can you guess who it is? The United Nations! Section E states that all viable agencies of the United Nations, including their personnel, facilities and resources, shall be transferred to the World Government and reconstituted. This section is a radical change from the previous Section D, which only invited the United Nations to transfer everything over to the World Government. Sounds like a prearranged deal to me! The World Constitution ends with a picture of the United Nations logo, which sums up their true agenda: "to control the whole world."

The contents of this document, "A Constitution for the Federation of Earth," are blatant enough that no further explanation is required, other than it goes hand in glove with the end-time scenario of Revelation 13. Will this World Constitution be the one Antichrist will use? Only God knows! For more information on the World Constitution, access their website at *www.wcpagren.org*.

There is one obstacle that is presently holding back the implementation of the World Constitution and New World Order. It is our God-ordained U.S. Constitution and Bill of Rights. In the very near future, these precious documents which have given Americans freedoms, liberties, and rights for over two centuries could be removed completely, suspended indefinitely, or bypassed with a stroke of a pen. There are three ways this could be accomplished.

The first way is through Executive Orders issued by the president, which appear in the *Federal Register* for thirty days. If there is no challenge by Congress, the order becomes law. Sadly, most American citizens do not know that our Republican form of government and the U.S. Constitution grants the president *no* lawmaking authority. Article 1, Section 8, states: "All legislative [lawmaking] powers herein granted shall be vested in a Congress. . . ."

When a president creates a new law by Executive Order, our representative government is completely averted and any concept of checks and balances or separation of powers is no longer involved in the legislative process. The bottom line is this: *Executive Orders give the president the power to act as an unaccountable dictator.*

Following are just a few of the shocking and frightening dictatorial powers that President Bill Clinton has created. Executive Order 12919[15] (Document C) gives the president complete power during a declared "State of National Emergency" (real or manufactured) over all food resources, food resource facilities, farms and farm equipment, fertilizer, all sources of energy, including gas and electricity, all transportation, including your personal car, highways, trucks, buses, trains, airports, jets, seaports, all health resources, including hospitals, health supplies and equipment, all metals and minerals, and all water resources. This is only one of three hundred Executive Orders President Clinton has issued. Most of them are nothing more than "power grabs" to bypass Congress and go directly to the Federal Emergency Management Agency (FEMA), or hand our national sovereignty to the United Nations, or give special rights to homosexuals and the environmentalists. One of Clinton's advisors, Paul Begala, smugly remarked: "Stroke of the pen. Law of the land. Kinda cool."[16] Future presidents will also have these same dictatorial powers at their fingertips. I wonder how many American citizens know how Hitler converted Germany's republic into a Nazi dictatorship in just three months. It was through Executive Orders.[17] Hitler also legalized abortion, euthanasia, homosexuals in the military, promoted environmental and animal rights, and passed thousands of laws and regulations that controlled every aspect of the German people's lives.[18] Finally, after Hitler had all the guns registered, he passed gun control laws to disarm the people, loaded them in railcars, and killed them in the Nazi death camps. Will America wake up before it's too late, or does she go down in history as the nation who followed Germany's footsteps and lost everything?

The second way our U.S. Constitution could be done away with is a Constitutional Convention. Let me set the stage by explaining what happened at the first and only Constitutional Convention.[19] At this Convention, held in Philadelphia, Pennsylvania, in 1789, our founding fathers threw out the existing government, which was the Articles of Confederation, and then wrote a totally new Constitution.

This first Convention also set up what is called a legal precedent. In other words, if another Constitutional Convention is called, the same thing could happen today. With the stroke of a pen, our government leaders could throw out our existing government and draft a new one.

A new constitution called the "Newstates of America Constitution"[20] (see *Foundational Documents of the New World Order*) has already been drafted by over one hundred liberal and prominent professors and attorneys. A tax-exempt foundation with the misleading name "Center for the Study of Democratic Institutions"[21] began writing this "abortive" constitution in 1964. This subversive constitution pretends to follow the language of our U.S. Constitution. It contains a preamble and twelve articles. According to the preamble, we are no longer called the United States of America, but the "Newstates of America." This goes right along with the New World Order!

In a nutshell, this Soviet-style constitution takes away our God-given unalienable rights. It gives us government privileges under a police state. Here are a few examples:

Article I, Section 8 states: "The practice of religion shall be privileged." Did you catch that? Privileged? A privilege is like your drivers license; it can be taken away. Section 8 also states, "but no religion shall be imposed by some upon others." Pastors, listen closely! Each time you preach, you impose your religion on others. Unless your preaching is politically correct and not considered a hate crime, will it be tolerated under the "Newstates Constitution"?

Section II states: "Education shall be provided at public expense only for those who meet appropriate tests of eligibility." I wonder what kind of "appropriate tests" there will be. Who will prepare them? You can be sure the revisionists and educrats will include situation ethics, values clarification, alternative lifestyles, and political correctness. Notice, there is nothing mentioned about private Christian schools or home-schooling. I wonder why? Because there will not be any Christian education unless it is state approved.

Article I, Section 8 under "Responsibilities" states: "There shall be a responsibility to avoid violence and to keep the peace; for this reason the bearing of arms or the possession of lethal weapons shall be confined to the police, members of the armed forces, and those licensed under law." This is complete federal gun control.

Article VIII, Section 14C states: "The Supreme Court may decide whether international law as recognized in treaties, United Nations agreements, or arrangements with other nations, has been ignored or violated." Once again America would be put at the mercy of the United Nations.

The other ten articles, when read closely, will set America up for a police state and under a dictator in the New World Order.

Maybe some of you are thinking our government officials would never allow the Newstates Constitution to replace our God-ordained U.S. Constitution. How many times have many of our leaders stated: "We need to reinvent government"? On March 4, 1993, President Bill Clinton stated: "We intend to redesign, to reinvent, to reinvigorate the entire national government."[22] Vice-President Al Gore stated: "What was written with quill pen is outdated and we need to reinvent government."

Let me tell you how close we are to calling for a Constitutional Convention! According to Article V of our U.S. Constitution, two-thirds, or thirty-four, of the states must call for a Constitutional Convention. Presently there are twenty-nine active calls on the books.[23] If five more states call for a Constitutional Convention, our existing U.S. Constitution could be thrown out. A new constitution could be approved or drafted.

The third way to do away with or suspend our U.S. Constitution is by martial law, when there is a declared State of National Emergency. Martial law is simply the rule of the military when the civil government can no longer maintain law and order. Under martial law, the Constitution is suspended and legal protections we enjoy such as *habeas corpus* (right to trial by jury) can be suspended and people can be arrested and imprisoned indefinitely without charges. All First Amendment rights such as freedom of speech, along with censorship of the press, TV, radio, and the Internet can be imposed. House to house searches and seizures of firearms could also be conducted.

A crisis, real or staged, can justify a State of National Emergency and martial law, for example, a financial collapse, nationwide bank run, terrorist attack, or a computer shutdown that causes the power grid, transportation, or banks to fail. In the 1992 Los Angeles riots, the people begged for martial law to stop the pain. In 1933 Americans yielded their freedoms to Franklin Roosevelt during the Great Depression when he declared a State of National Emergency. In that same year, the German people willingly surrendered their freedom to Adolph Hitler in a State of National Emergency *after* Hitler and his Brown Shirts burned the German parliament and blamed it on the communists.[24]

The bottom line is, the legal authority for martial law and the suspension of our U.S. Constitution is in place through Executive Orders.

The military machinery is also in place through the Department of Defense plan, "Operation Garden Plot."[25] This plan from the Department of Defense links the American military units with the United Nations military to assist each other during civil disturbances by a resistance group, religious organization, or other persons considered to be nonconformists. This linking of the American military with the United Nations military leads us to the second world system in Revelation 13, the world military. Let's read the last two questions in verse four: "Who is like unto the beast? Who is able to make war with him?

The first question, "Who is like unto the beast?" makes it clear there has never been anyone like the beast, the Antichrist. He will come on the world scene with hypnotic charm and charisma. At first, the Antichrist will be the world's most prominent, powerful, and popular personality. According to the books of Daniel and Revelation, he will be an intellectual, oratorical, political, commercial, and military genius. One of the greatest achievements by the Antichrist, or the symbolic rider on the white horse (Rev. 6:2), will be world peace. This false or counterfeit peace will be short-lived, according to Revelation 6:4. In order to bring about this world peace and later to stage a fight at the Battle of Armageddon, the Antichrist will need a world military. This leads us to the second question in Revelation 13:4, "Who is able to make war with him?" This question makes it clear that no nation on earth will be able to make war with the Antichrist's world military and win.

Chapter 3

World Military

There is already an international organization which has a world military, right in our front yard, in America. They have their headquarters in Manhattan's East Side in New York City. In 1946, multimillionaire John D. Rockefeller, Jr., gave a gift of $8.5 million for the sixteen-acre tract of land.[26] The United States gave a $65 million interest-free loan for construction of the three buildings,[27] which includes the thirty-nine-story glass and marble Secretariat Building, the low-domed General Assembly Building, and the rectangular Conference Building. The Ford Foundation added a $6.6 million gift for the library,[28] and New York City gave adjacent land with deeded streets and waterfront rights along the East River.[29] Recently, multimillionaire Ted Turner gave a gift of $1 billion to this organization.[30] I am sure most of you know about what I am speaking — *the United Nations.*

Before we discuss the details of the United Nations world military, I want to first give you some of its history, background, and agenda. The U.N. was born in 1945 in San Francisco. Originally, this organization of fifty nations was to be a forum for countries to discuss their differences in the name of peace. From the very start, it has been nothing more than a Trojan horse. Its first secretary-general, Alger Hiss, a U.S. State Department official, was exposed, convicted, and sentenced to prison as a Soviet spy.[31] Virtually all secretary-generals since have also been Soviets.[32]

The one hundred eighty-one articles of the United Nations Charter and Statute of International Court of Justice [Document D] does not mention the name of God, nor does it reflect any of the Christian values and principles found in the Declaration of Independence

The United Nations System

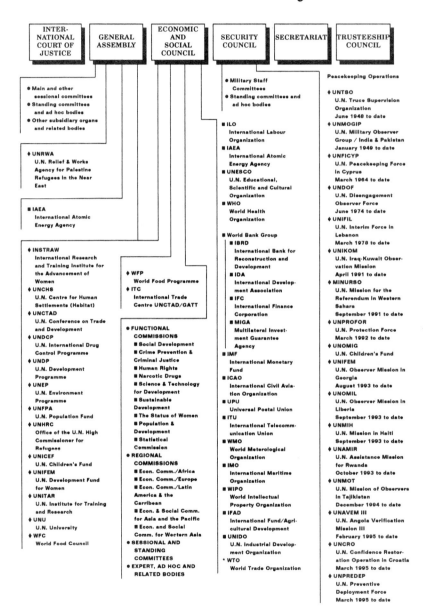

INTER-NATIONAL COURT OF JUSTICE	GENERAL ASSEMBLY	ECONOMIC AND SOCIAL COUNCIL	SECURITY COUNCIL	SECRETARIAT	TRUSTEESHIP COUNCIL

● Main and other sessional committees
● Standing committees and ad hoc bodies
● Other subsidiary organs and related bodies

♦ UNRWA
U.N. Relief & Works Agency for Palestine Refugees in the Near East

■ IAEA
International Atomic Energy Agency

♦ INSTRAW
International Research and Training Institute for the Advancement of Women
♦ UNCHS
U.N. Centre for Human Settlements (Habitat)
♦ UNCTAD
U.N. Conference on Trade and Development
♦ UNDCP
U.N. International Drug Control Programme
♦ UNDP
U.N. Development Programme
♦ UNEP
U.N. Environment Programme
♦ UNFPA
U.N. Population Fund
♦ UNHRC
Office of the U.N. High Commissioner for Refugees
♦ UNICEF
U.N. Children's Fund
♦ UNIFEM
U.N. Development Fund for Women
♦ UNITAR
U.N. Institute for Training and Research
♦ UNU
U.N. University
♦ WFC
World Food Council

♦ WFP
World Food Programme
♦ ITC
International Trade Centre UNCTAD/GATT

● FUNCTIONAL COMMISSIONS
■ Social Development
■ Crime Prevention & Criminal Justice
■ Human Rights
■ Narcotic Drugs
■ Science & Technology for Development
■ Sustainable Development
■ The Status of Women
■ Population & Development
■ Statistical Commission
● REGIONAL COMMISSIONS
■ Econ. Comm./Africa
■ Econ. Comm./Europe
■ Econ. Comm./Latin America & the Carribean
■ Econ. & Social Comm. for Asia and the Pacific
■ Econ. and Social Comm. for Western Asia
● SESSIONAL AND STANDING COMMITTEES
● EXPERT, AD HOC AND RELATED BODIES

● Military Staff Committee
● Standing committees and ad hoc bodies

■ ILO
International Labour Organization
■ IAEA
International Atomic Energy Agency
■ UNESCO
U.N. Educational, Scientific and Cultural Organization
■ WHO
World Health Organization

■ World Bank Group
■ IBRD
International Bank for Reconstruction and Development
■ IDA
International Development Association
■ IFC
International Finance Corporation
■ MIGA
Multilateral Investment Guarantee Agency
■ IMF
International Monetary Fund
■ ICAO
International Civil Aviation Organization
■ UPU
Universal Postal Union
■ ITU
International Telecommunication Union
■ WMO
World Meterological Organization
■ IMO
International Maritime Organization
■ WIPO
World Intellectual Property Organization
■ IFAD
International Fund/Agricultural Development
■ UNIDO
U.N. Industrial Development Organization
* WTO
World Trade Organization

Peacekeeping Operations

♦ UNTSO
U.N. Truce Supervision Organization
June 1948 to date
♦ UNMOGIP
U.N. Military Observer Group / India & Pakistan
January 1949 to date
♦ UNFICYP
U.N. Peacekeeping Force in Cyprus
March 1964 to date
♦ UNDOF
U.N. Disengagement Observer Force
June 1974 to date
♦ UNIFIL
U.N. Interim Force in Lebanon
March 1978 to date
♦ UNIKOM
U.N. Iraq-Kuwait Observation Mission
April 1991 to date
♦ MINURSO
U.N. Mission for the Referendum in Western Sahara
September 1991 to date
♦ UNPROFOR
U.N. Protection Force
March 1992 to date
♦ UNOMIG
U.N. Children's Fund
♦ UNIFEM
U.N. Observer Mission in Georgia
August 1993 to date
♦ UNOMIL
U.N. Observer Mission in Liberia
September 1993 to date
♦ UNMIH
U.N. Mission in Haiti
September 1993 to date
♦ UNAMIR
U.N. Assistance Mission for Rwanda
October 1993 to date
♦ UNMOT
U.N. Mission of Observers in Tajikistan
December 1994 to date
♦ UNAVEM III
U.N. Angola Verification Mission III
February 1995 to date
♦ UNCRO
U.N. Confidence Restoration Operation in Croatia
March 1995 to date
♦ UNPREDEP
U.N. Preventive Deployment Force
March 1995 to date

♦ United Nations programmes and organs (representative list only)
■ Specialized agencies and other autonomous orgs. within system
● Other commissions, committees, and ad hoc and related bodies
* Coop arrangement between U.N. and WTO are under discussion

or our United States Constitution. That alone should be a wake-up call for every patriotic and God-fearing American. In spite of our godly heritage, the U.S. Senate ratified the U.N. Charter in 1945. In the past fifty-plus years, the United Nations system has become much more than just a forum for discussion between nations. As we look at the U.N. structure and its principle organs, we can see a distinct governmental structure which includes the International Court of Justice (Document D) or the World Court, located at The Hague in the Netherlands. The two thousand-plus seat General Assembly discusses issues on war and peace and also makes recommendations on all matters within the scope of the U.N. Charter. The Economic and Social Council includes the World Trade Organization, the International Monetary Fund, and the World Bank. The Security Council's primary responsibility is maintaining international peace and security through peacekeeping operations.

The Secretariat employs over five thousand men and women inside its thirty-nine-story building who prepare reports and issue press releases. The most sinister of all U.N. organs is the International Criminal Court. The Court was established in Rome in 1998. Presently, ninety nations have signed the International Criminal Court document, and five have formally ratified it. If ratified by the U.S. Senate, American individual protections and immunities, which are guaranteed by the Bill of Rights, would be utterly nullified. The International Criminal Court will work hand-in-glove with the World Constitution and world police, which we discussed earlier.

In the last few decades, the United Nations empire has lain the foundations for global values, global security, global development, and global governance. These global policies are being enacted through treaties and international laws which have been drafted at U.N. summits, programs, conventions, and conferences. For example, in the mid-1980s entrance signs to national parks and monuments around the world suddenly announced those areas had been designated by the United Nations as "Man and the Biosphere Reserves," or "World Heritage Sites." After much protest, the words

"United Nations" were removed from some of the signs. These reserves and sites are the brain child of the United Nations Educational Scientific and Cultural Organization.

As of June 1995, there were three hundred twenty-four U.N. Biosphere Reserves in eighty-two countries around the world,[33] with forty-seven U.N. Biosphere Reserves and twenty U.N. World Heritage Sites in the United States.[34] Just a few include: Grand Canyon National Park, Yosemite National Park, Sequoia and Kings Canyon National Park, Yellowstone National Park, Glacier National Park, Death Valley National Monument, Big Bend National Park, Carlsbad Caverns National Park, Mammoth Cave National Park, Rocky Mountains National Park, Great Smoky Mountains National Park (which encompasses parts of six states), Independence Hall, the Statue of Liberty, and fifty-four other U.N. national parks and monuments.

Looking closely at the U.N. Biosphere Reserve signs, you will see the occult symbol "ankh." It is located above and between the large letters M and a. The *Dictionary for Mysticism* defines the ankh as the "Egyptian cross, shaped like a capital T with an oval loop on the top, symbol of life in occult tradition."[35] It was "used by the gods as an instrument for awakening the dead to a new life."[36] "The Crux Ansata (or ankh) was frequently observed in the hands of the old kings and gods of Egypt. . . ."[37]

A former witch reveals that the ankh is

> . . . an emblem to identify the wearer as a worshipper of the sun god Ra, a seeker of the Satanist beliefs, and one who practices the worship to the unknown gods of the supernatural. The wearer acknowledges the sun god Ra, works the voodoo of the unseen world through this hex.[38]

According to the National Park Service, the World Heritage symbol located at the top of the World Heritage signs

. . . symbolizes the interdependence of cultural and natural properties. The central square is a form created by man and the circle
represents nature, the two being intimately linked. The emblem
is round, like the world, but at the same time it is a symbol of
protection.[39]

Once again we can see the New Age philosophy in the definition of
the World Heritage symbol.

Amazingly, our precious American parks and monuments were
designated by the U.N. without congressional approval or public in-

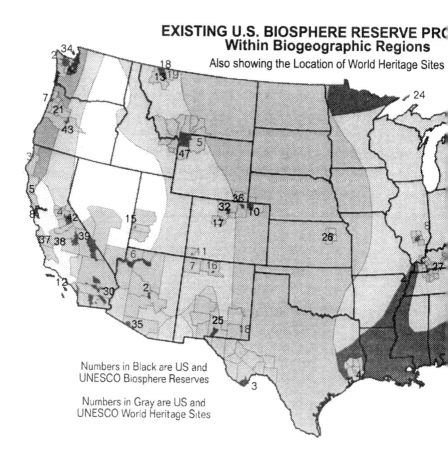

EXISTING U.S. BIOSPHERE RESERVE PRC
Within Biogeographic Regions
Also showing the Location of World Heritage Sites

Numbers in Black are US and
UNESCO Biosphere Reserves

Numbers in Gray are US and
UNESCO World Heritage Sites

put.[40] According to Representative Helen Chenowith, who testified before the House Committee on Resources, June 10, 1997, "over fifty-one million acres in the United States have been designated as either Biosphere Reserves or World Heritage Sites."[41] To date, there is no direct evidence that UNESCO has ever dictated national policy concerning any Biosphere Reserves or World Heritage Sites in the United States. However, a delegation from the United Nations in 1995 indirectly stopped the development of a gold mine located about five miles from the northeast corner of Yellowstone National Park.[42] The mine, according to the Clinton administration, alleged-

NAMES OF BIOSPHERE RESERVES

1. Aleutian Islands, AK
2. Beaver Creek, AZ
3. Big Bend, TX
4. Big Thicket, TX
5. California Coast Ranges, CA
6. Carolinian-South Atlantic, SC, GA
7. Cascade Head, OR
8. Golden Gate, CA
9. Central Gulf Coastal Plain, FL
10. Central Plains, CO
11. Champlain-Adirondack, NY/VT
12. Channel Islands, CA
13. Coram, MT
14. Denaili, AK
15. Desert, UT
16. Everglades, FL
17. Fraser, CO
18. Glacier, MT
19. Glacier Bay-Admiralty Island, AK
20. Guanica, Puerto Rico
21. H. J. Andrews Experimental Forest, OR
22. Hawaiian Islands, HI
23. Hubbard Brook, NH
24. Isle Royale, MI
25. Jornada, NM
26. Konza Prairie, KS
27. Land Between the Lakes, KY
28. Luquillo, Puerto Rico
29. Mammoth Cave Area, KY
30. Mojave and Colorado Deserts, CA
31. New Jersey Pinelands, NJ
32. Niwot Ridge, CO
33. Noatak, AK
34. Olympic, WA
35. Organ Pipe Cactus, AZ
36. Rocky Mountains, CO
37. San Dimas, CA
38. San Joaquin, CA
39. Sequoia-Kings Canyon, CA
40. South Atlantic Coastal Plain, NC
41. Southern Appalachian VA, WV. KY, TN, NC, SC, GA, AL
42. Stanislaus-Toulumne, CA
43. Three Sisters, OR
44. University of Michigan, MI
45. Virgin Islands National Park and Hassel Islands
46. Virginia Coast, VA
47. Yellowstone, WY, MT, ID

NAMES OF WORLD HERITAGE SITES

1. Wrangell-St. Elias NP, Glacier Bay (AK)
2. Olympic NP (WA)
3. Redwood NP (CA)
4. Yosemite NP (CA)
5. Yellowstone NP (WY)
6. Grand Canyon NP (AZ)
7. Chaco NHP (NM)
8. Cahokia Mounds Site (IL)
9. Mammoth Cave NP (KY)
10. Statue of Liberty (NY)
11. Mesa Verde (CO)
12. Independence Hall (PA)
13. Monticello (VA)
14. Great Smoky Mts. NP (TN, NC)
15. Everglades NP (FL)
16. Pueblo de Taos (NM)
17. Hawaii Volcanoes NP (HI)
18. Carlsbad Caverns NP (NM)
19. Glacier NP (MT)
20. La Fortaleza & San Juan (Haiti)

A small sampling of the United States National Parks that have been named as part of the UNESCO "Program on Man and the Biosphere." Notice the Egyptian ankh in the MAB logo.

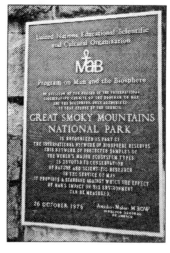

The World Heritage emblem symbolizes the interdependence of culture and natural properties; the square is a form created by humankind and the circle represents nature, the two being intimately linked. The emblem is round like the world and at the same time it is a symbol of protection.

Ankh variations

Isis and Amon each holding an ankh

Ra (or Re)   Sebek

ly put Yellowstone National Park, a "World Heritage Site," in danger. The gold mine company was already in compliance with both state and federal guidelines. Yellowstone National Park superintendent Mike Finley stated:

> As ratified by Congress, the provisions of the World Heritage Treaty have the force and statutory authority of federal law. By inviting the committee to visit the park and assess the mine's potential impacts, the Interior Department acted as it was legally required to do.[43]

In August 1995, a presidential decree materialized in the *Federal Register* which more than quadrupled the affected acreage.[44] Nineteen thousand acres were to be declared off-limits to mining permits in what was called "Greater Yellowstone Ecosystem." Environmental attorney William Pendley warned: "IF the U.N. is given power to set policy in Yellowstone and the region, property rights will be in peril throughout the Western United States."[45]

The real and future agenda for the Biosphere Reserves and all major ecosystems of the World Heritage Sites is revealed in a 1,140-page document entitled "Global Biodiversity Assessment."[46] This assessment came out of the 1992 United Nations Convention on Biological Diversity. President Bill Clinton signed the Biodiversity Treaty in 1994. The original treaty was only eighteen pages. On September 30, 1994,[47] hours before the U.S. Senate was poised to ratify the U.N. Biodiversity Treaty, a draft copy of the GBA was obtained, even though the U.N. said "no draft of the document existed."[48] This provided the "smoking gun" that removed the treaty from floor consideration. Section 13.4.2.2.3 stated:

> . . . representative areas of all major ecosystems in a region need to be reserved, that blocks should be as large as possible, that buffer zones should be established around core areas, and that corridors should connect these areas. The basic design is central to the re-

Global Biodiversity Assessment

V.H. Heywood, Executive Editor   **R.T. Watson**, Chair

UNEP

Published for the United Nations Environment Programme

CAMBRIDGE
UNIVERSITY PRESS

cently proposed Wildlands Project in the United States by Reed
Noss in 1992, a controversial . . . strategy to expand natural habi-
tats and corridors to cover as much as thirty percent of the U.S.
land.[49]

To get the big picture of the Wildlands Project, the June 25, 1993,
issue of *Science* magazine calls for 23.4 percent of America's land to
be put into wilderness and 26.2 percent into corridors and human
buffer zones.[50] Unbelievably, this is almost fifty percent of our land!

The Wildlands Project is largely the work of Dave Foreman, principle founder of "Earth First."[51] He summarizes the project as a
bold attempt to grope our way back to 1492.[52] John Davis, editor of
Wild Earth, the official publication of the Wildlands Project, stated:
"The Wildlands Project seeks nothing less than the end of industrial civilization . . . everything civilized must go. . . ."[53]

We can get an approximate idea of what fifty percent of America
will be like if the Global Biodiversity Treaty and Wildlands Project
is implemented. The simulated maps[54] of the U.S. found on the following pages were produced by Dr. Michael S. Coffman, who received
his B.S. in forestry, his M.S. in biology, and his Ph.D. in forest science. He is a respected scientist and ecologist who has been involved
in ecosystem research for over twenty-five years in both academia
and industry. He taught courses and conducted research in forest
ecology and forest community dynamics for ten years at Michigan
Technological University. While there, he published a book on forest ecosystem classification in upper Michigan and northern Wisconsin, which has become the standard for classification in the region. He also assisted the U.S. Forest Service in developing an ecological land classification system for each of the national forests in
Region 9.

During his tenure with the paper industry, Dr. Coffman became
chairman of the Forest Health Group within NCASI (National Council for the Paper Industry for Air and Stream Improvement), a respected scientific research. In this, and other related responsibili-

ties, he became intimately involved in such national and international issues as acid rain, global climate change, wetlands, cumulative effects, and biological diversity.

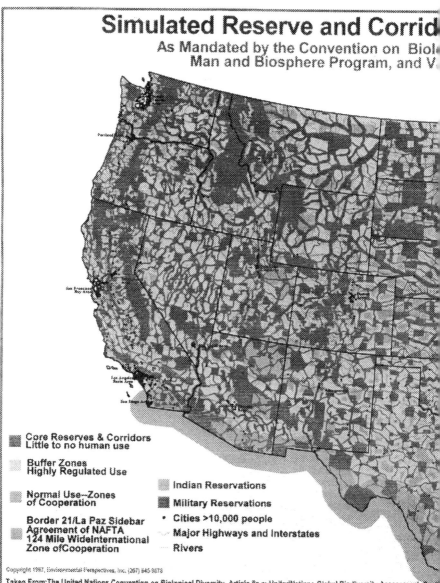

Simulated Reserve and Corrid

As Mandated by the Convention on Biol Man and Biosphere Program, and V

Core Reserves & Corridors
Little to no human use

Buffer Zones
Highly Regulated Use

Normal Use--Zones
of Cooperation

**Border 21/La Paz Sidebar
Agreement of NAFTA
124 Mile WideInternational
Zone ofCooperation**

Indian Reservations

Military Reservations

• **Cities >10,000 people**

Major Highways and Interstates

Rivers

Copyright 1997, Environmental Perspectives, Inc. (207) 846-9878

Taken From:The United Nations Convention on Biological Diversity, Article 8a-e; UnitedNations Global Biodiversity Assessment, Secti
Also see Science, "TheHigh Cost of Biodiversity," 25 June, 1993, pp 1968-1871 and the Border 21 Sidebar of NAFTA. The very high per

Dr. Coffman is currently president of Environmental Perspectives, Inc., and CEO of Sovereignty International. Environmental Perspectives provides professional guidance and training in defin-

ystem to Protect Biodiversity

)iversity, The Wildlands Project, UN and US
JN, US Heritage Programs, and NAFTA

US Man and the Biosphere Strategic Plan, UN/US Heritage Corridor Program, "The Wildlands Project", WildEarth.
iffer zone in the West isdue to the very high percentage of federal land. Do not use for real estate purposes.

ing environmental problems and conflicts and developing solutions to specific issues. Sovereignty International helps many different organizations to bring a positive message of how national sovereignty, free market enterprise, private property rights, and traditional values are superior to global treaties and agreements being proposed by the United Nations. He played a key role in stopping the ratification of the Convention on Biological Diversity (Biodiversity Treaty) in the U.S. Senate by anticipating and exposing the unbelievable agenda behind the treaty.

These maps reveal the proposed Core Reserves and corridors represented by the large dark areas with little to no human use. The corridors which connect the biosphere reserves will be fifty miles wide. The human buffer zones, represented in the large lighter area, will be highly regulated with severely limited human use. The small slightly darker area represents the protected islands where people will live. The small black dots represent cities with ten thousand people. This is an enlarged map showing how our land will be used for the re-wilding of America. The bottom line to the "Wildlands Project," if implemented, is that virtually all private property rights as we know it would be abolished. Interestingly, the first plank of the Communist Manifesto is the abolition of private property.

The question is, will you and your family have to relocate because of the "Wildlands Project" and the United Nations Global Biodiversity Treaty? As already stated, President Clinton has signed the Biodiversity Treaty, even though the U.S. Senate would not ratify it. Despite the Senate's refusal, the Clinton administration is gradually implementing the provisions of the treaty through Executive Orders and bureaucratic fiat.[55] Two of those Executive Orders are No. 12852[56] entitled "President's Council on Sustainable Development," and Executive Order 12986[57] entitled "International Union for Conservation of Nature and Natural Resources."

Here are two examples out of many of how far the radical environmentalists want to go. First, an article dated March 7, 2000, on the front page of the *Washington Times* states:

Walking through the forest is harmful to the environment, according to a proposed rule by the Forest Service. . . .

. . . Critics say the broad language could halt all future road
building.

These people want to return the forest to the conditions existing before the Europeans landed on the continent, said Sen. Frank
H. Murkowski, Alaskan Republican and chairman of the Energy
and Natural Resources Committee.

The controversial proposal would severely restrict recreational
use such as mountain biking, snowmobiling, skiing, all-terrain
vehicles, and rock climbing.

A second article entitled "Recreation Criticized as Environmental
Threat" by David Brown, executive director of America Outdoors,
states:

Richard Knight, a professor of wildlife conservation at Colorado
State University, was quoted as stating that recreational use is a
greater threat [to the environment] than mining and logging.

Knight is not alone in promoting this point of view. A recent
article in *Bio-Science* (vol. 46) by Elizabeth Losos of the Smithso-
nian Tropical Research Institute and four other scientists ranked
recreation as second only to water projects as pushing species toward threatened or endangered status. Off-road vehicles, skiing,
swimming, and hiking were among the activities cited as having
an adverse threat. Federal agencies are openly entering the debate. The Bureau of Land Management in Colorado sponsored a
conference in early June titled, Recreation: Promise or Peril in
the West. Speakers included Scott Silver from Wild Wilderness.
Silver believes that the agency budget cuts are part of a clever plot
by conservatives to usher in a takeover of public lands by corporate sponsors.

It is clear to see that our parks and forests are becoming off limits to
American citizens. The last time you visited a park, did you notice

that many of them have "No Fishing," "No Hunting," and "No Trespassing" signs?

Not content with just our national land treasures, President Clinton has launched another land grab assault on the American people. By presidential proclamation, which allow for no (as in none) opposition by the American people or Congress, Bill Clinton has instituted as law the "American Heritage Rivers Initiative" (AHRI).[58]

Under this initiative, American rivers, their tributaries, and all adjacent wetlands, are to receive special attention from the federal government. The definition of wetland was so vague that it included many pieces of property with small, shallow, seasonal puddles. The government repeated the pattern by using the protection of wildlife (including microbes, rats, and tiny fish) to control private property.[59] AHRI will gain control of our rivers from respective state governments and then place them under thirteen planned federal agencies who will enforce a program to preserve natural, historic, cultural, social, economic, and ecological diversity.

This is all happening through gradualism, which simply means a principle used to achieve social or political change by almost imperceptible steps or degrees.

Slowly, but surely, through gradualism our national parks, national monuments, forests, rivers, tributaries, and surrounding wetlands are being controlled by our federal government. Much of our private property is also being controlled by high taxation, zoning, and radical environmental protection laws. What is going to be left for us and our children?

Sadly, while this nation, collectively and individually, is mesmerized by silly TV sit-coms, unending sports programs, materialism, and the Internet, gradualism is methodically and secretly taking away our God-given rights and also our American privileges and liberties.

Wake up America!!!

There is still more, much more. The *Global Biodiversity Assessment* states in Section 12.2.3 that

Christianity [has] gone the farthest in setting humans apart from nature . . . and that, before Christian traditions, people viewed themselves as members of a community — living and nonliving, such as plants, animals, rocks, springs, pools, trees, birds, and mountain peaks. Thus, rivers may be viewed as mothers; animals may be treated as kin and thus antelopes are brothers to followers in India.[60]

This is nothing less than a pagan and New Age worldview. Have you noticed the similarities between the GBA and the Earth Charter which we discussed earlier? The GBA goes on to say, "When cultures began to convert to Christianity . . . they began to cut down the sacred groves to bring the land under cultivation."[61] Recall in the Old Testament, the groves[62] or high places were where human sacrifices were committed and false gods were worshipped, and all manner of abominations were carried out under the domination of satanically-inspired leaders! Sadly, many of these people have reestablished the sacred groves and named them "safety forests" instead.[63]

GBA also lists items deemed to be non-sustainable and detrimental to global biodiversity. They include grazing of livestock, fencing of pastures, modern agriculture, paved and tarred roads, railroads, modern hunting, harvesting of timber, logging, fossil fuels used for driving various kinds of machines, dams, reservoirs, power line construction, private property, population growth, sewers, pipelines, golf courses, ski runs, and scuba diving.[64] Believe it or not, there are more items deemed non-sustainable. Section 11.2.3.2 of the GBA explains:

A reasonable estimate for an industrialized world society, at the present North American material standard of living, would be one billion. At the more frugal European standard of living, two to three billion would be possible.[65]

This means the elimination of three to five billion people. The fifteen hundred-plus scientists and experts who drafted the GBA are not the only ones calling for radical population reduction. Here are just a few examples of many . . .

Dr. Sam Keen, a New Age writer, made the following statement at a State of the World Forum held in San Francisco by the Gorbachev Foundation U.S.A. in 1996: "Cut the population by ninety percent and there aren't enough people left to do a great deal of ecological damage."[66] That eliminates four and a half billion of the present six billion people alive on planet Earth.

The late Jacques Cousteau wrote in the November 1991 issue of the *United Nations Educational, Scientific and Cultural Organization,* ". . . this is a terrible thing to say. In order to stabilize the world population, we must eliminate 350,000 people per day. It is a horrible thing to say, but it's just as bad not to say it."[67]

On one of the highest hilltops in Elberton, Georgia, stands four huge granite stones referred to as the Georgia Guidestones,[68] or the American Stonehenge. Engraved in eight different languages on the

Georgia Guidestones

four stones are Ten Guides or commandments. The first of the guides on this Druid-like monument reads: "Maintain humanity under 500,000,000 in perpetual balance with nature." Once again, there is a call to eliminate five and a half billion people. The other nine guides on the monument promote world government, the environment, and spirituality. Since 1979, the Georgia Guidestones have been used for occult ceremonies and mystic celebrations.

The bottom line to the *Global Biodiversity Assessment* that came out of the 1992 U.N. Earth Summit meeting in Rio de Janeiro is to invert the biblical view of man's relationship to the environment. In Genesis 1:26 God commanded man to "have dominion over the fish of the sea, and over the fowl of the air, and over the cattle, and over all the earth, and over every creeping thing. . . ." Verse 28 commanded man to subdue the earth, which means to "bring into subjection." God put man at the center of the universe and the animals, plants, trees, and water under his control. Man is also commanded to be a proper steward of the earth and its resources. I am for clean air, water, soil, and protecting wildlife, provided I have more rights than the environment and the animals. It is clear that the United Nations Biodiversity Treaty wants to *reverse* the God-ordained purpose of *man* being at the *center* of the universe. The treaty puts the *environment* and the *animals* at the *center.* Romans 1:22–23, 25 states:

> Professing themselves to be wise, they became fools, And changed the glory of the incorruptible God into an image made like to corruptible man, and to birds, and four-footed beasts, and creeping things. Who changed the truth of God into a lie, and worshiped and served the creature more than the Creator. . . .

Other global policies being set by the United Nations include the 1994 U.N. Convention on Population Development,[69] held in Cairo Egypt. This convention was about international abortion rights. The 1994 U.N. World Conference on Women,[70] held in Beijing, China, was headed up by First Lady Hillary Rodham Clinton from the United States group. The delegates and activists attacked traditional marriages and redefined the word family to include same-sex marriages. They also expanded the word gender to five groups, including homosexual, bisexual, transsexual, male, and female.

In 1996 the U.N. Conference on Human Settlements[71] was held in Istanbul, Turkey. This conference was also called Habitat II. Habitat means "dwelling place," and refers to where we live. Sustainable development was the main goal of this meeting. They discussed sustainable cities, sustainable transport, and sustainable families.

The U.N. holds five thousand conferences a year.[72] We have only discussed a few. It is evident that the U.N. is a vehicle for control of the people, land, resources, and sovereignty of the world. Guess which member of the U.N. empire pays the most dues for their fifteen-billion-dollar-a-year budget.[73] Sadly, the hard-earned tax dollars of U.S. citizens are used to pay twenty-five percent,[74] or almost four billion dollars of the U.N.'s budget. U.S. contributions to the U.N. over the last fifty years are estimated to be ninety-six billion dollars.[75] Will America wake up in time to see the rope which has been purchased with her own dollars and now is being placed around her neck?

Now that we have the history, background, and agenda of the U.N., let's discuss how our American government helped the U.N. become a world military. At the Sixteenth General Assembly of the U.N., the United States introduced a "Program for General and Complete Disarmament in a Peaceful World." This nineteen-page document was entitled "Freedom from War — Department of State Publication 7277"[76] (see *Foundational Documents of the New World Order*). On page three, the following shocking statement is found:

> The overall goal of the United States is a free, secure, and peaceful world . . . a world which has achieved general and complete disarmament under effective international control . . . in accordance with the principles of the United Nations.

The program goes on to explain the three stages of how the United States and all national armies will disarm. The first and second stage would establish a permanent international peace force within the United Nations, reduce the armies of the world and at the same time strengthen the U.N. peace force. It would also eliminate weapons of mass destruction and "the dismantling or the conversion to peaceful uses of certain military bases and facilities." This fits the closing of many American military bases such as the Presidio in San Francisco.

The third stage calls for the states to provide agreed manpower for the U.N. peace force, disbanding all national armed forces. No state would have the military power to challenge the progressively strengthened U.N. peace force. This would supposedly assure peace in a disarmed world. Something very frightening happened when an American soldier announced he would not wear the U.N. uniform or serve U.N. commanders. Army Specialist Michael New,[77] a committed Christian, decorated for his service in the Persian Gulf, was court-martialed for refusing to join a U.N. unit in Macedonia. Soon no one will be able to make war with the United Nations. Once this happens, the stage will be set for the world dictator, Antichrist, to walk on the scene and "who is able to make war with him" according to Revelation 13:4. During the last three and a half years of the Tribulation period, the world military will "make war with the saints and overcome them" (Rev. 13:7).

The United Nations must have a world military to accomplish their central and main goal, world peace. To the casual observer, world peace sounds very lofty and noble, but for the most part, it is only a storefront for their real agenda . . . world control and domination.

The very first line of Article I of the Charter of the United Nations (Document D) states its purpose: "to maintain international peace and security." The remaining one hundred and ten articles, including the preamble, use the word peace thirty-six times, and twenty-three of those times the phrase "international peace and security" is used. *Webster's Dictionary* defines the word "security" as "safety." Recall the Word of God gives us a warning concerning false peace and safety in First Thessalonians 5:2–3. We also know the Bible teaches in Daniel 7:27 that there will not be true world peace until Jesus the Messiah returns and sets up His everlasting kingdom.

I want to take you on a sightseeing tour of the U.N. headquarters located in New York City. You will see their vision of world peace and safety does not include the Prince of Peace, Jesus Christ, the only begotten Son of God. When you walk inside the General Assembly building, there is a huge stained-glass window right outside the Meditation Room entitled "Peace and Man." The window depicts all mankind from around the world. What is very shocking is a picture of a large serpent in the center of mankind. Recall the serpent deceived Eve in the Garden. Likewise, the U.N. is deceiving the world with false peace and safety.

A large mural inside the Security Council symbolizes the promise of future peace. Another mural depicts man's struggle for peace. Two more murals in the Delegate's Lobby also depict peace. As you step outside the U.N. building, there is a Japanese peace bell in a Shinto-like shrine. In the North Garden is a statue entitled "We Shall Beat Our Swords Into Plowshares." This portion of Bible scripture from Isaiah 2:4 is etched on a wall of the U.N. It is evident that their intent is to beat your sword and my sword into plowshares, but not theirs.

Still another work of art is a hand gun with the barrel tied in a knot. This represents gun control. If you conduct a little research on the history of gun control, you will be horrified to find fifty-six million people have been murdered by their own government in the twentieth century.[78] This atrocity happened after the peoples' guns were taken away. They include twenty million from the Soviet Union, one and one half million in Turkey, thirteen million in Germany, twenty million in China, one hundred thousand in Guatemala, three hundred thousand in Uganda, and one million in Cambodia. In

America we are heading quickly toward complete gun control. Recall the old saying, "Those who forget history are doomed to repeat it." It is plain to see we need criminal control in America, not gun control.

The final peace symbol at the United Nations is a statue of a rider on a horse with a bow-like object in his hand. This statue is simply labeled "Peace." The rider is holding the world in his right hand, which represents worldwide peace.

Interestingly, Revelation 6:2 symbolizes a rider on a white horse with a bow. This rider represents the world's false peace movement and is also a counterfeit of the true rider on a white horse in Revelation 19:11. This true rider is none other than the King of Kings and Lord of Lords, Jesus Christ. Only with the return of Jesus Christ the Messiah will true and everlasting peace be established.

The United Nations is also a very spiritual organization. Robert Muller, a Catholic and lawyer-economist, began his work at the United Nations in 1948 and was assistant secretary-general until 1984. He believes and supports the concept of a one-world government united with a one-world religion, and that the U.N. should be the entity empowered to achieve this goal. He writes:

> Was it not inevitable that the U.N. would sooner or later acquire a spiritual dimension. . . . I have come to believe firmly today that our future peace, justice, fulfillment, happiness, and harmony on this planet will not depend on world government, but on divine or cosmic government, meaning that we must seek and apply the natural, evolutionary, divine, universal, or cosmic laws which must rule our journey in the cosmos.[79]

In another book by Muller entitled *My Testament to the U.N.,* he favorably quotes the following prophecy by Chinmoy regarding the United Nations' ultimate destiny:

> No human force will ever be able to destroy the United Nations, for the United Nations is not a mere building or a mere idea; it is

not a manmade creation. The United Nations is the vision-light of the Absolute Supreme, which is slowly, steadily, and unerringly illuminating the ignorance, the night of our human life. The divine success and supreme progress of the United Nations is bound to become a reality. At his choice hour, the Absolute Supreme will ring in his own victory-bell here on Earth through the loving and serving heart of the United Nations.[80]

Muller has also stated he would "like to see published someday a Bible which would show how the United Nations is a modern biblical institution. . . ."[81] Muller has gone so far as to refer to the U.N. as "the body of Christ"[82] — a view shared by Chinmoy, who describes the organization as "the chosen instrument of God . . . a divine messenger carrying the banner of God's inner vision and outer manifestation."

Chinmoy Kumar Ghose is a Hindu mystic who leads the United Nations meditation group.

Speaking of meditation, you will recall the mural outside the Meditation Room entitled "Peace and Man" with the large serpent in the center of mankind. Robert Muller has a whole chapter on "Prayer and Meditation at the United Nations" in his book *New Genesis, Shaping a Global Spirituality*. He also states that some have "found God" at the United Nations, referring to mystic Dag Hammarskjøld of Sweden, former Secretary-General of the United Nations (1953–1961). Muller continues in this chapter that U Thant of Burma (Secretary-General, 1961–1971) "was a Buddhist whose religion does not believe in God and yet was one of the most spiritual persons I have ever known."

Even rule number sixty-two of the "Rules and Procedures of the General Assembly" invited the representatives to observe one minute of silence dedicated to prayer or meditation.

Interestingly, the United Nations Meditation Room has *ten* wicker benches against the corridor wall.[83] Recall that Daniel 7:24 calls for *ten* world leaders or kings, and so does the "World Constitution." Just a coincidence???

The large stone altar in the middle of the Meditation Room has a meditation light shining on it. The stone altar is four feet high and is a block of crystalline iron ore from a Swedish mine which weighs six and a half tons.[84] This is the largest crystal of its kind ever mined. I might add that crystals are very popular in the New Age movement.

Hammarskjøld directed a leaflet to be written about the Meditation Room and stated the following about the stone altar: ". . . it [stone altar] is dedicated to the God whom man worships under many names and in many forms."[85] Welcome to the World Religion crowd!!!

Chapter 4

World Religion

The third world system found in Revelation chapter thirteen is a world religion. Verse eight states: "And all that dwell upon the earth shall worship him. . . ." In order for all of the people on earth to worship the Antichrist there must be a worldwide religion. This world system will be run by the second beast, the False Prophet.

I want to give you a brief history of how the world's religion and spiritual traditions have united together in a global movement. The first worldwide attempt in America to bring all the religions of the world together was held at the first "Parliament of World Religions" in 1893 in Chicago. It was the largest conference of its kind in the history of the world up to that time. The Parliament even called itself "Babel . . . the actual beginning of a new epoch."[86] Hindus, Buddhists, Muslims, Roman Catholics, Protestants, and a host of others prayed and dialogued for seventeen days.

Just a few of the speech titles included "Worship of God in Man," "Brotherhood of Man," "The Good in All Faiths," "Sacred Books of the World," "The Ultimate Religion," "Ethics of Christian Science," and "Shinto." The ultimate apostate of the 1893 Parliament of World Religions was speaker Annie Besant, editor of the monthly publication, *Lucifer Magazine*.[87] The founder of *Lucifer Magazine* and the Theosophical Society was none other than the infamous Helena Blavatsky.[88] From 1887 to 1897, Blavatsky's Theosophical Society, along with Annie Besant, published, promoted, and circulated *Lucifer Magazine*.[89] They were also well known in the Woman's Masonic movement of that time.[90]

Another well known follower of Blavatsky was Adolph Hitler. This evil revolutionary kept a copy of Blavatsky's 1,474-page occult

LUCIFER

THEOSOPHICAL MONTHLY

DESIGNED

To bring "to light the hidden things of darkness."

"I, Jesus . . . . am the bright, the Morning Star," (φωσφόρος — *Lucifer*)
—*vide* 2 Peter i. 19 *and* Rev. xxii. 16.

The Light-bearer is the Morning Star or Lucifer; and "Lucifer is no profane or Satanic title.
It is the Latin *Luciferus*, the Light-bringer, the Morning Star, equivalent to the Greek φωσφόρος
. . . the name of the pure, pale herald of daylight."—YONGE.

EDITED BY

H. P. BLAVATSKY and ANNIE BESANT

London : The Theosophical Publication Society, 7, Duke Street, Adelphi, W.C.

Boston : The Occult Publishing Co., 120 Tremont Street, Room 35, Boston, Mass

New York : W. Q. Judge P.O. Box 2659

[ENTERED AT STATIONERS' HALL ALL RIGHTS RESERVED.]

classic *The Secret Doctrine* at his bedside.[91]

Of the major Theosophists, Alice Bailey was probably the most instrumental in developing the infrastructure of today's New Age movement. In 1922 Bailey founded the Lucifer Publishing Company in New York City.[92] Two years later she changed the name of Lucifer Publishing Company to Lucis Trust.[93] By 1949, Bailey had compiled twenty-four occult books, most of which were written in a trance through her spirit guide, Djwhal Khul.[94] In reality, Djwhal Khul was a lying and seducing spirit or demon, according to Deuteronomy 8:9–12 and First Timothy 4:1. Bailey died on December 15, 1949, just thirty days after she claimed her spirit guide had finished writing through her.

Lucis Trust was headquartered at 866 United Nations Plaza for twenty years.[95] They even maintained the U.N. Meditation Room.[96] Finally, in the 1980s, after receiving some unexpected adverse publicity, Lucis Trust moved to a new location on the twenty-fourth floor at 120 Wall Street in New York. Today, Lucis Trust is a global organization with a membership of about six thousand, with three main planetary centers in New York, London, and Geneva. They are also on the roster of the United Nations Economic and Social Council.[97] The Theosophical Society is also a global organization, with its international headquarters in Pasadena, California, and overseas agencies in Australia, Finland, Germany, the Netherlands, South Africa, Sweden, and the United Kingdom.

In 1988 a special committee was formed to commemorate the one hundredth anniversary of the Parliament of World Religions. Its charge was to organize the largest gathering of religious leaders in history for this Parliament.

In 1993 the one hundredth anniversary of the original Parliament of World Religions was held again in Chicago. Guess who showed up? Representatives of Lucis Trust and Blavatsky's Theosophical Society.[98] Also in attendance were the major religions, along with voodoo and Druid priests, wiccans (witches), Satanists, snake charmers, sun worshippers, Freemasons, Celtics, occultists, neopagans, and an assortment of other inter-religions.[99] Altogether, approximately fifty-five hundred religious leaders and another eight hundred fifty-seven individuals from the press were blinded by the god of this world and the father of lies.

The most significant event of the nine-day Parliament, with over five hundred seminars, lectures, and workshops, was the endorsement of a document titled "Toward a Global Ethic."[100] This document calls for a global and sustainable world order through a common set of core values found in the teachings of all religions. God has already given us a set of global ethics in the Ten Commandments and the Beatitudes.

All the world's religious dignitaries signed and agreed that the "Global Ethic" (Document E) represented the beginning of a true one-world religion. In comparison, the Global Ethic will be to religion what the Earth Charter is to global government.

Still another giant step toward a world religion took place on June 25, 1997, at Stanford University in San Francisco. This meeting was titled "United Religions Initiative 2000."[101] Sitting down together were two hundred delegates and leaders from the world's religions and spiritual traditions. The attendance included everyone from Australian aborigines and California pagans to Christian ecumenical leaders. The main goal of this global movement was to bring all the world's religions to a common table and design a United Nations Religions Charter, which they hoped to be a reality in the year 2000.[102] This meeting was coordinated by Robert Muller, who has been involved with thirty-two specialized agencies of the United Nations for more than thirty years. Recall he has also held the title of Assistant Secretary-General. Muller stated, "My greatest personal dream is to get a tremendous alliance between all the major religions and the U.N."[103]

Although Muller is the visionary for the United Religions, the Rev. William Swing of Grace Episcopal Cathedral in San Francisco is the main figurehead and spokesperson. In a press release, Bishop Swing stated: "The United Religious Initiative, if successful, will be a spiritual United Nations. And what better place to give it birth than the Bay Area, which gave birth to the present U.N."[104] Guess where United Religions is located. At the Presidio, in the Thoreau Center for Sustainability, along with the Gorbachev Foundation and the United Nations Resource Center, just like three peas in a pod.[105] A person would have to be blind not to see all the pieces of the New World Order puzzle coming together.

Many of the same people, organizations, and agendas keep popping up in each world system. The many different documents, charters, conventions, conferences, and treaties which we have discussed are no more than a smokescreen to usher in the New World Order.

To solidify the unification of the world's religions, the International Religious Foundation has published *World Scripture: A Comparative Anthology of Sacred Texts*.[106] The founder and author is the Reverend Sun Myung Moon of Korea. This 882-page *World Scripture* is a spiritual smorgasbord of just about every religion, belief, tradition, and sacred text under the sun. Just a few include the *Tibetan Book of the Dead, Epistle to the Son of Wolf, Apocrypha, Bhagauad Gita, Koran, Book of Mormon, Kabbalah, Veda, Lotus Sutra,* and *even* the Holy Scriptures of the Christian Bible. Still other beliefs and teachings are about Mother Earth, Grandmother Moon, Father Sun, Grandfather Sky, witchcraft, shamanism, New Age, ritual use of tobacco through a sacred pipe (allowing one to communicate with spirits), rituals of the sweat lodge, reincarnation, karma, purgatory, rosary, yin-yang, and near-death experiences. After hearing this kind of information from the *World Scripture,* a red warning flag should go up in the spiritual heart of every born-again, blood-washed, spirit-filled Christian. The texts, beliefs, teachings, and experiences which I have given you are nothing less than the extra-biblical revelation which violates Revelation 22:18–19. Jesus Christ, the King of Kings and Lord of Lords, who is seated at the right hand of the Father and is God incarnate, warned that many false prophets and doctrines of devils would come in the last days. The *World Scripture* is a prime example. Jesus Christ also stated, "I am the way, the truth, and the life: no man cometh unto the Father, but by me" (John 14:6). Once again, we need to love and pray for the multitudes of lost, sincere souls who have "a way which seemeth right unto a man, but the end thereof are the ways of death" (Prov. 14:12).

The stage is being set for the False Prophet to walk on the scene and put the finishing touch on the unification of the world's religions. That finishing touch is described in Revelation 13:11–15. Here we find the False Prophet will be in charge of getting *all* the people who dwell on the earth to worship the Antichrist. To help persuade the multitudes, the False Prophet will perform great wonders and miracles, which in turn will deceive everyone.

Apparently the Antichrist will somehow receive a deadly wound and perform a fake resurrection to counterfeit Christ's resurrection (Revelation 13:3, 12). According to Second Thessalonians 2:4, the man of sin, or Antichrist, will then set himself up in the rebuilt Temple of God in Jerusalem proclaiming he is God. Once these events occur, the False Prophet will have an image set up. Anyone that refuses to worship the image of the Antichrist will be killed. This refusal will probably be labeled as a hate crime. Presently we are seeing how hate crimes are being used against Christians in the public arena.

Chapter 5

World Economy

The False Prophet will not only be in charge of the world religious system, but also of the world economic system. This fourth system is spoken of in Revelation 13:16–18:

> And he [False Prophet] causeth all, both small and great, rich and poor, free and bond, to receive a mark in their right hand, or in their foreheads: And that no man might buy or sell, save he that had the mark, or the name of the beast, or the number of his name. Here is wisdom. Let him that hath understanding count the number of the beast: for it is the number of a man; and his number is six hundred threescore and six.

The main subject in these verses describes the mark of the Beast, which we will discuss shortly. In verse seventeen we read that "no man might buy or sell." This means there must be a world economic system. To properly understand how the world economic system will come together, we need to go back about twenty-six hundred years to Daniel chapter two. In this passage, Daniel, by Divine intervention, gives the interpretation of King Nebuchadnezzar's dream. In verses twenty-eight through forty-five Daniel sweeps down through the corridors of time. He gives a panoramic view of how four Gentile world empires will come on the scene, starting in his time and concluding in the latter days. The four Gentile world empires were represented by the great image in King Nebuchadnezzar's dream.

When we research ancient history, we find Daniel's prophecies were right on target. Babylon was the first world empire, represent-

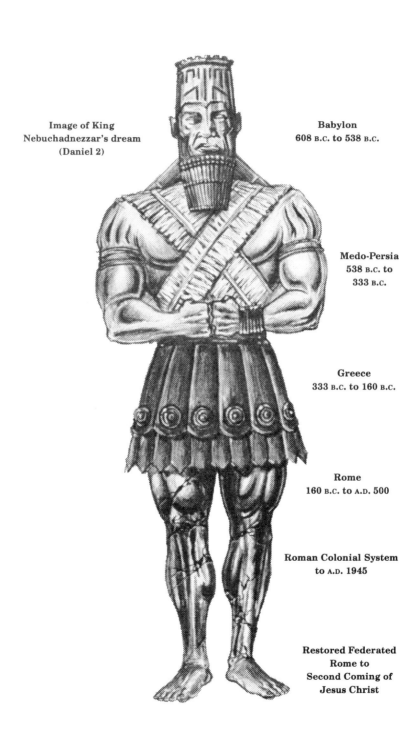

Image of King
Nebuchadnezzar's dream
(Daniel 2)

Babylon
608 B.C. to 538 B.C.

Medo-Persia
538 B.C. to
333 B.C.

Greece
333 B.C. to 160 B.C.

Rome
160 B.C. to A.D. 500

Roman Colonial System
to A.D. 1945

Restored Federated
Rome to
Second Coming of
Jesus Christ

ed by the head of gold, which fell to the Medes and Persians in 538 B.C., represented by the breast and arms of silver. The Medo-Persian Empire fell to the Greek Empire in 333 B.C., represented by the belly and thighs of brass. Finally, the fourth empire, Rome, conquered the Greek Empire about 160 B.C., represented by the legs and feet of iron and clay.

The Roman Empire was never conquered by an outside army. However, it started to crumble from within around A.D. 476 to A.D. 500. Since Rome was never really conquered, that means there will be a revived Roman Empire in the last days. Many have tried to bring the Roman Empire back together, but have failed. Charlemagne, Napoleon, Bismarck, and even Hitler tried. The reason they failed: it was not in God's timing.

In 1992 the old Roman Empire came back together through the formation of the European Economic Community. Even the headline from the 1992 *European* magazine read, "Back Together Again." When were these nations together in the first place? In the old Roman Empire, so, even the Europeans understand this is a revival of the Roman Empire. The original treaty, signed in 1957, established the European Community. It was called the Treaty of Rome, and was signed in Rome. The handwriting is on the wall!

Here is an official poster circulated and published by the Council of Europe in Brussels, one of the three main divisions of the EEC. It portrays a fifteenth century drawing of the Tower of Babel. Notice the slogan at the bottom right of the poster, "Europe — Many Tongues, One Voice." Now look at the modern-day crane atop the Tower of Babel. Together the slogan and crane symbolically tell us that the EEC will complete a one-world order, which Nimrod failed to accomplish back in

Genesis chapter eleven. Recall that Nimrod said their Tower of Babel would reach unto heaven. Look closely at the stars on the EEC poster. Do they look a little strange? These stars are inverted, or upside-down, standing on one point. The stars on our U.S. flag always stand on two points. The stars on the EEC poster are called in the occult the Goat of Mendes satanic stars. The points at the top represent the horns of the goat, the points on the side represent the ears of the goat, and one point on the bottom represents the beard of the goat.

In Matthew 25:31–41, Jesus symbolically calls Christians sheep, who will inherit everlasting life, and non-Christians are called goats, who will be cast into everlasting fire prepared for the devil and his angels.

The Goat of Mendes satanic star is also found on the cover of the Satanic Bible, written by the late Anton LaVey, who was the high priest of the First Church of Satan in California. Anton LaVey is pictured, with the Goat of Mendes star behind him. A rock group named Venom also has the satanic goat star on the cover of their album *Welcome to Hell*.

The outline of the Goat of Mendes star can clearly be seen in two of the Pokémon monsters, Alakazam and Kadabra. Maybe that is why six hundred eighty-five people in Japan went into epileptic seizures while watching the Pokémon cartoon.[107]

Another nine-year-old boy had stolen money from his mother's purse to buy more Pokémon cards. The boy later confessed he had heard the devil urging him to do it. The boy burned his cards and also warned his friends.[108]

There are eleven Goat of Mendes stars above the Tower of Babel. Ten stars are the same size, but one is larger and sits above the rest, indicating its headship over the other ten stars. Recall that God's Word tells us in Daniel 7:24 that in the last days ten kings shall arise out of the fourth kingdom. Then another king shall arise and rule over the ten original kings. This is the same symbolic message portrayed in the EEC poster. The Club of Rome has divided the world into ten political and economic regions which it refers to as kingdoms.[109] Also remember, the World Constitution calls for ten world magna regions, ten world capitals, ten world commissioners, and a world senior administrator.

Following are some pictures of the new Euro dollars created by the European Monetary Union.[110] On the front left side of the Euro is a blank space. No one in the public arena knows what will be

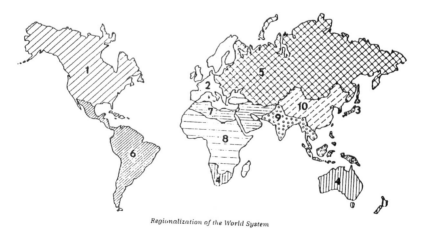

Regionalization of the World System

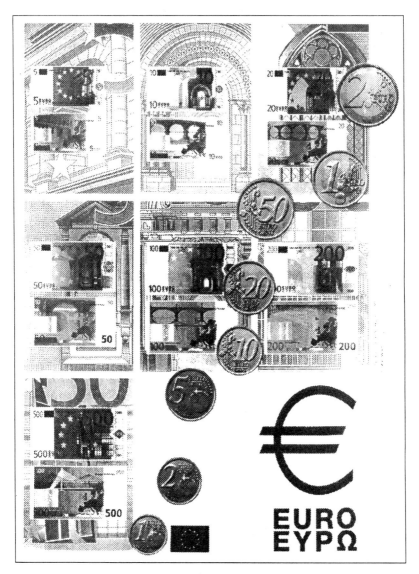

printed or shown here. Other currency around the world has the same open space, such as England's pound, France's franc, Australia's dollar, and German's mark. What is more fascinating: found on the back of all the Euro dollars is a map of the old Roman Empire. Will the present European Monetary Union which makes up the old Roman Empire become the one-world economic system run by the

False Prophet? Only God knows for sure, but the answer might be found in a statement made by one of the founders and leaders of the EEC. Belgian foreign minister Henrii Spaak stated:

> We do not want another committee. We have too many already. What we want is a man of sufficient stature to hold the allegiance of the people and lift us up out of the economic morass into which we are sinking. Send us such a man and be he God or devil, we will accept him.[111]

Once the False Prophet takes charge of the world's economy, he will need to identify, track, and locate the billions of people who have or have not taken the mark of the Beast. The technology for this kind of global surveillance is now possible through super computers. In case you have not been following the advanced development of these super computers, let me bring you up to date.

In 1976, Cray Research of Minneapolis, Minnesota, created the Cray-I super computer, costing fifteen million dollars. This computer could crunch anywhere from one hundred fifty million to two hundred million calculations per second. Today, that same Cray-I is considered a dinosaur and a wimp.

Next came the Cray-II super computer, which could calculate billions of transactions per second. This computer generated so much heat, it had to be immersed in liquid nitrogen to keep its processors from melting. Now, it too has been thrown into the bone yard.

The newest, fastest, and most powerful super computer in the world is called Blue Mountain,[112] located at the Los Alamos National Laboratory in New Mexico. The name Blue Mountain came from the forty-eight refrigerator-high blue boxes, or slaves, that make up the backbone of this monster computer. Blue Mountain has a peak speed of 3.1 teraflops, or 3.1 trillion calculations per second. Their goal is a one hundred teraflop computer by 2004, and soon after that a petaflop super computer which will calculate one quadrillion transactions per second. This kind of advanced technology and knowledge reminds us of the end-time prophecy of Daniel 12:4: ". . . knowledge shall be increased."

Dr. Jas Mercer-Smith, director of the Los Alamos Laboratory, made this chilling statement: "I'm here to save the world. We created the most horrible weapons imaginable and the result is unprecedented peace."[113] Once again, this kind of peace reminds one of the false peace which Antichrist will bring into the world.

Most of us have heard rumors about the alleged Beast computer, housed at the European Common Market headquarters in Brussels, Belgium. Contrary to these rumors, the greatest concentration of highly advanced super computers are located right here in America at the National Security Agency in Fort Meade, Maryland, situated between Washington and Baltimore.

As a matter of fact, out of the one hundred ninety-four most powerful computer sites on earth, the NSA is number one.[114] The NSA, a federal agency, was born in silence without congressional debate by a presidential directive, signed by then-president Harry Truman, on October 24, 1952. The NSA is the largest and most secret intelligence agency of the U.S. government. Its two original and main functions were to protect U.S. government communications

NSA's new $47 million supercomputer facility at Ft. Meade, Maryland. Opened October 1996. Internet photo.

National Security Agency headquarters (circa 1957 when the NSA opened), Ft. George G. Meade, Maryland. Photo credit: Department of Defense.

and to intercept foreign communications.

Today the NSA occupies one thousand acres, which includes its massive headquarters with seven million square feet of office space, its Public Affairs office, and its new forty-seven million dollar super computer facility.[115] Below the NSA's headquarters operations building in the cavernous subterranean expanses of the earth, which stretches for city blocks, are ten acres of underground Cray super

NSA Complex, courtesy of NSA's Public Affairs Office, Ft. Meade, Maryland.

computers.[116] These super computers are tied together with fifty-two separate computer systems used throughout the world.[117] That's not all. The four super huge microwave dishes located there serve as the downlink site for information beamed by global positioned satellites from NSA's many worldwide field sites.

In addition to NSA's super computers and global positioned satellites is the Biometric Consortium,[118] also located in Fort Meade. The Biometric Consortium web page opens with the following statement: "The Biometric Consortium serves as the U.S. Government's focal point for research, development, test, evaluation, and application of biometric-based personal identification/verification technology."

Notice the Biometric Consortium is the U.S. government's focal point for personal identification and verification technology. The word "biometric" is defined as "automated methods of verifying or recognizing the identity of a living person based on physiological or behavioral characteristics." This would include everything from hand geometry to retinal, voice, and facial patterns. When we tie together the Biometric Consortium's personal identification and verification technology with NSA's ten acres of underground super computers which can calculate up to trillions of transactions per second, it's time to ask a question. Where could this super technology lead us? The following quote by Senator Frank Church, the former chairman of the Senate Intelligence Committee, regarding the NSA surveillance capabilities pretty much confirms everyone's fears:

> At the same time that capability could be turned around on the American people and no American would have any privacy left, such as the capability to monitor everything: telephone conversations, telegrams, it doesn't matter. There would be no place to hide. If this government ever became a tyranny, if a dictator ever took charge in this country, the technological capacity that the intelligence community has given the government could enable it to impose total tyranny, there would be no way to fight back. . . . We must see to it that this agency [NSA] and all agencies that possess this technology operate within the law and under proper supervision, so that we never cross that abyss. That is the abyss from which there is no return.[119]

Should we be surprised by Senator Frank Church's statement made over a quarter of a century ago? If you are a student of the Bible, the senator's words were rather prophetic. The Holy Scriptures tell us that during the seven-year Tribulation period, there will be a tyrannical world dictator, the Antichrist. Just imagine how he will use this technology for evil! There will be no place to hide from his world police, super computers, global positioning satellites, or sophisticated biometric technology. We are truly seeing a sneak preview of the future Antichrist-led tyranny, the abyss from which there is no return, as Senator Church stated.

Recently, Georgia Republican Bob Barr led a congressional movement to force the NSA to answer for spying on U.S. citizens. This global spy system, known as Echelon,[120] can capture everything from phone calls to e-mail to faxes. Congressional hearings on Echelon are expected early this year.

Former NSA analyst Wayne Madsen stated that Echelon is basically a system based on key words in a conversation or key words in an e-mail. Those key words of interest are basically preprogrammed in something called a "dictionary." According to Madsen, this dictionary may be searching your phone calls, faxes, and e-mails to sniff out terrorists, hackers, and other potential threats.

Retired intelligence officer Mike Frost spent nineteen years collecting top-secret information at Canada's Communications Security Establishment (CSE), Canada's equivalent of America's National Security Agency. Frost was asked how deep Echelon can go into someone's life.

> As far as you want to go, Echelon can go into your private life — that includes your private life with your doctor, your minister, your lawyer, your stock broker, your wife, your girlfriend, your children, your business partner, your business enemies — as far as they want to go.

Both the United States and Canada officially deny that this massive spy network even exists. But Frost showed CBN News a station in Ottawa where such interceptions are part of the daily routine.

Intelligence experts say Echelon is only one of many tools Big Brother can use to listen in on your life. In fact, government agencies can literally pull your personal information out of the air — without ever touching your computer. The procedure is code-named "Tempest"[121] and it's a trick Frost learned from the NSA. By simply aiming an antenna at your computer monitor, intelligence experts can use the radiation emitted by the monitor to reconstruct the images on your screen. No hacking, no passwords!!!

Once again, soon "there will be no place to hide."

Now that technology is available for the future False Prophet to keep track of every person on earth, half of his work is already completed. The other half of his work will be the positive identification of every person on earth. This will be accomplished by the yet-future mark of the Beast.

Before we discuss the mark of the Beast, I want to give you some information on positive identification systems. YMCA is using "hand-recognition" systems to keep track of its members in at least twenty states across the country.[122] The member simply places his or her hand on the Hand-Key's pad while a built-in camera snaps three

20 AUTOMATIC I.D. NEWS   CASE-STUDY   AUGUST 1994

Hand-recognition system shapes up access control

Local YMCA replaces membership cards with high-tech handshake

BY JOHN JESITUS, CONTRIBUTING EDITOR

The YMCA in Ashland, OH, wasn't happy with its membership system. Management wanted a better way to track its 3,000 members, so it turned to a high-tech handshake for its solution.

The YMCA has been using a bio-

Vertical pegs on the identification pad ensure proper placement of Ashland YMCA members' hands on the access control system.

metric system which recognizes a person's entire hand since November. Chris Braden, business manager there, says, "Prior to implementing this device, our members used to have membership cards. And it was very difficult getting them to bring their cards, or remember to bring them. So a lot of times, people would come and go, [and] we didn't know if they were members or not.

As membership grew, Braden says, "It just became more and more difficult to keep track of who's who," a problem exacerbated by fairly quick staff turnover. During busy periods in particular, the club had no way of knowing who really belonged there and who didn't. Moreover, since the facility's paper ID cards listed only names and expiration dates, Braden says, "they didn't serve any purpose," particularly since people weren't required to bring them to the YMCA anyway.

For these reasons, almost two years ago, club management began searching for a system that would help it track and control facility access. Management investigated bar-coded ID cards and picture identification technology (which uses video images of members' faces) before learning of a system called the HandKey system through industry-related advertisements. And among the three solutions, Braden says, the YMCA chose the HandKey because it felt it was the best, easiest and most efficient answer to the site's problems.

Setup and installation

Last July, the YMCA bought a HandKey system and MACS (Membership Access Control System) software directly from ATM Technologies, which distributes the HandKey system for manufacturer Recognition Systems. The system also required the

John Jesitus is a freelance technical writer and former editor of Communications News.

purchase of a Plus Data 386 DX40 PC with 4M of memory and a 120M hard drive, as well as a CTX International SuperVGA color monitor, both supplied by local reseller Advanced Computer Technology (ACT).

Along with explaining the new hardware's computer language to the user, ACT owner Jim Gordon, working with phone support from ATM, was instrumental in connecting the Hand-Key to the 386 computer and installing a relay necessary to unlock the Ashland facility's main door (while other arrangements are possible, all three pieces of equipment reside in a small lobby outside the YMCA's main doors, with the monitor and Hand-Key sitting atop the computer on a counter).

Probably the most time-consuming setup step, however, involved creating initial system records. Braden says. "It took a lot of time to get our membership into the system before we could actually start using it."

Prior to installing the Auto ID system, the YMCA stored all of its membership information in a home-grown computerized billing system. And while many such programs can download much accounting information directly into ATM's software, loading such data into Ashland's setup required the user to print a hardcopy list and manually key in each person's name and membership type, along with other vital information including addresses and expiration dates. Each person's three- or four-digit PIN (personal identification number) was assigned in the same way. Braden says, "It just took a lot of man-hours to do that."

Meanwhile, the YMCA sent letters to its clients informing them of the pending change and asking them to take a few minutes during their next visit to have their hands photographed for system records. To do this, a member simply places his or her hand on the HandKey's pad while a built-in camera snaps three shots, one each of the top and either side of their hand. These pictures are averaged into a single three-dimensional computerized composite for storage in system records.

Then, on subsequent visits, users who want to access the YMCA can simply punch their PIN numbers into the HandKey's keyboard and, when prompted, place their hands on the unit's hand pad. Unlike finger- or thumbprint identification systems, which may fail to take accurate readings if clients turn their digits or press them onto pads too softly, vertical pegs located on the HandKey's pad ensure that members' mitts are situated for optimal reading. Also unlike fingerprint systems, says ATM, the Hand-Key scores first-read rates in the upper 90% range even if users' hands are sweaty or if the members themselves use or gain weight (instead of using static images, the system updates these files each time a member uses it).

The entire recognition process takes about 1.5 seconds. Once the system makes a match, a door buzzer sounds, and the person has four sec-

onds in which to open it for access to the YMCA's swimming pools, weight rooms and other facilities.

Acceptance and advantages

While children took to the new technology instantly, often racing each other to get to the HandKey first, Braden says, a few of the club's members at first were hesitant because they feared that the YMCA would indeed be working with records of their hand or fingerprints. Others members who had been using the club for 10 and 20 years without such access control procedures balked as well.

But once the YMCA cleared up misconceptions and explained how the system would help both the club and its members, Braden says, nearly every one got behind it. In this area, the most obvious advantage is non-members no longer can enter the facility. While it's nearly impossible to attribute hard-dollar savings to such advances, Braden says that, in addition to keeping peace among club users, barring strangers from the YMCA helps people feel better about on-site safety, both in regards to their valuables and to the many children who use the facility. In a few instances, the system also has helped management deny access to kids who have been troublemakers.

Similarly, whenever a member uses the system, it logs the date and time of entry into its records. Having access to such data has made it much easier for the YMCA to track traffic on its corporate memberships in which members may be reimbursed by their employers if they make a minimum number of visits per month.

At the same time, the biometric ID system prevents members from passing access cards to unauthorized friends and others. And in contrast to what often happened under the user's former system, nobody's left their hand at home yet.

Indeed, the hand recognition system is working so well that the only change Braden anticipates is the addition of more members. While the user's current hardware can accommodate up to 4,000 people, routine computer-chip upgrades will enable it to grow still further in the future.

For now, Braden says her company has experienced no problems with the system, a fact she finds somewhat surprising considering that the YMCA only recently became familiar with such technology. "It's just like anything—you have to learn it," she says. "And the best way is hands-on."

For more information circle Reader Inquiry Card
ATM Technologies .... (W.) 300
Advanced Computer Technology ... (W.) 301

Biometric systems suit many areas

Biometric access control system at Ashland YMCA lets members enter while also allowing non-member entrance.

Hand-recognition ID systems are becoming more common in settings from prisons and private concerns to computer rooms and college cafeterias. In comparison to other forms of biometric identification including those which use fingerprints, voice recognition and retinal scanning, supporters of ID systems that rely on the uniqueness of users' hands say that such technology is more reliable and user-friendly.

Health clubs are a fairly recent entrant in the biometric user circle. In fact, ATM Technologies, distributor of the HandKey hand recognition system, began considering the possibility of swapping ID cards commonly used in health centers for fingerprint or voice-based technology just last year, in response to user complaints about the hassles created by bar-coded ID cards (ATM has more than 100 card-based installations of its access control software in the field).

Voice technology would have proven unreliable due to heavy traffic and background noise health clubs tend to generate, explains ATM President Alan McGaffin. Fingerprint identification got the thumbs-down too after several months of testing since read rates were compromised if members had too much sweat or even hand lotion on their digits.

With hand recognition added to its system, ATM found first-read rates were high and access was quickly granted. While fingerprint systems take about three seconds to grant access, the hand recognition system cut this time in half.

Since ATM's HandKey solution hit the market last May, it has been installed in some 20 YMCAs around the country.

In the not-too-distant future, McGaffin says standard network links could enable large fitness chains including Bally's to link multiple sites operating up to 100 secured doors in total. Interfaces to time-and-attendance software also soon bring the benefits of biometric identification to labor tracking applications in businesses from bodybuilding to banking.

YMCA

Ashland YMCA, Ashland, OH.
Industry:
Access control.
Benefits:
• Recognition takes only 1.5 seconds.
• Non-members no longer enter facility.
• Safer place for members.
• Easy to track corporate membership use for billing credits.
• Forgotten, lost, transferred membership card problem eliminated.

photos. The entire recognition process takes about one and a half seconds.

ATM Technologies president Alan McGaffin stated: "In the not too distant future . . . such products [hand-recognition systems] . . . may soon bring the benefits of biometric identification . . . in businesses from bodybuilding to banking."[123]

Hand-recognition systems are also being used to help detect welfare fraud in California.[124]

All this emerging hand-scan technology seems to have one thing

Hand Images Help Detect Welfare Fraud

HUMAN SERVICES — LOCAL/STATE
$50,000 instead of $1.2 million
By Brian Miller, Features Editor

"There is no way to tell how much duplicate aid is going on."

FOR AUTOMATED DATA CAPTURE SYSTEMS USERS

VOLUME 11, NO. 8 • AN ADVANSTAR PUBLICATION

JULY 1995

A defaced face can't beat the heat

Thermal faceprints provide new kind of secure automatic ID

BY JOHN BURNELL, NEWS DIRECTOR

WASHINGTON, DC —A "hot" new technology that never forgets a face is the newest form of personal automatic identification. If you're one in a million, there are 5,000 people in the world just like you—except that your face releases heat in a pattern as unique as your fingerprint. The heat-release pattern can be recorded and analyzed with a new system from Technology Recognition Systems (TRS), which will use the technology to develop highly secure biometric identification systems.

The system uses an infrared video camera to take a thermal picture, called a thermogram, of a face. Software processes the image and makes the recognition based on analysis of the vascular system facial tissue and skin heat emissions. The system, which has been demonstrated but is not yet available, can capture and process the image within six seconds. Perspiration, bruises, swelling, and even plastic

SEE FACIAL HEAT PAGE 18

System displays unique thermal facial characteristics...

...which it uses to identify a face in six seconds.

Thermal faceprints are hot new ID method

FACIAL HEAT CONTINUED FROM PAGE 1

surgery or disguises won't change an individual's heat emission pattern.

"The applications for this technology are endless. We envision a day when consumers won't need cards at ATMs, high level telephone communications can be fully secured and newborns can be protected before leaving the hospital through the creation of private family records," said David Evans, president and CEO of TRS. "Ear and nose temperatures aren't

included in the analysis because they are highly sensitive to temperature changes. The infrared camera is insensitive to light and produces accurate images in total darkness from up to four feet away, although range could be extended. Evans insists the technology is more accurate than other biometric identification techniques, such as digital fingerprinting, voice prints or retina scanning. "In most applications you don't have to change the way you operate," said Evans.

Despite the advanced software, the system can run from a 386 PC. Digitized thermograms require between 2K and 4K to store.

The first commercial product to incorporate the technology will be an access control system, scheduled for release next spring. TRS will pursue eight applications during the next five years: access control, computer security, identification credentials, credit card security, communications security, private records and law enforcement support. ■

For more information circle Reader Inquiry Card
Technology Recognition Systems   CIRCLE 310

18 AUTOMATIC I.D. NEWS

in common — it is all designed for the *right* hand.

Thermal faceprints[125] are a hot, new ID method. The system for thermal faceprints uses an infrared video camera to take a thermal picture, called a thermogram. Neither surgery nor disguise will change a person's heat emission pattern.

Retinal identification technology is also available. "Eyedentification systems"[126] read the unique, unalterable retinal pattern of an individual's eye. It is virtually foolproof.

Sprint has unveiled a smart phone card that relies on your voice imprint as security protection. Dave Schmeig, president of Sprint's consumer service group, said "The 'Voice Fonecard'[127] was designed to prevent fraud. . . ." A spokesman later added that the card would work even if the customer was tired or ill and the voice was slightly different than normal. The reason for this is because the card's owner will have his or her voice imprint memorized by Sprint's computer.

It is so clear to see how the multitudes are being primed for the end-time and yet-future positive identification of the mark of the Beast.

There have been so many interpretations of the mark of the Beast and the six hundred, threescore, and six. Therefore, I would like to give the original Greek meanings. The Greek word for mark is *charagma*, which means "to scratch or to sharpen to a point," like an engraver's tool. From this description, could John the Revelator in his Patmos vision have seen a hypodermic needle? A tool which when sharpened to a point can make a small scratch in the skin. One of the cross references for the Greek words used for six hundred, threescore, and six, is *chi xi stigma*, and means not only 366 as a numeral, but also to "stick or prick for recognition of ownership" or "a mark incised." If we add to this definition, verse sixteen states that the mark will go *in*, not on, the right hand, and *in*, not on, the forehead. Could John the Revelator have seen a microchip implant which will go under the skin by means of a hypodermic needle? Also remember the definition included the phrase "a mark incised." The front part of a microchip is called an incisor. Very interesting and sobering!

This kind of technology is already being used in animals and humans. It all began so innocently during the late 1980s, when approximately fifteen million stray animals a year were being put to sleep when their owners could not be found. The solution — microchip implants. Following are just a few examples of many. In St. Louis, a news article describes the "Mane Event,"[128] park rangers horses being injected in their necks with microchips. In the past month, the Humane Society of Missouri has put chips in seventy-five hundred newly adopted pets. A *San Francisco Chronicle*[129] article tells of cats being microchipped between their shoulder blades. New York City has a high-tech pet locator in the form of a microchip

ST. LOUIS/REGION

◄ SATURDAY, JUNE 3, 1995 ►

Mane Event

County Rangers Get Their Horses Microchip IDs

By Diane M. Targovnik
Of the Post-Dispatch Staff

Queen Elizabeth II's dog has one and, now, so do the St. Louis County park rangers' horses.

They're sporting a 96-bit microchip injected into their necks to help identify lost or stolen pets.

Each chip — about the size of a grain of rice — has a unique number that can be found with a hand-held scanner. That number will identify the veterinarian who has the animal's records or, if the owner paid extra, it will make the animal's address available from a nationwide database.

In the past month, the Humane Society has put chips in 7,500 newly adopted pets.

On Friday, six rangers' horses got free Avid-brand chips from their veterinarian, Dr. Chris Rolf. The horses did not have to be sedated.

The chips are a big change from the old way of identification. Jerr Wilson, a park ranger with the St. Louis County mounted unit, said: "Before, we had diagrams of the horses with their markings to identify them — if we could find the diagrams."

Chips have been around for about 10 years, although only recently have they become popular.

In the past month, the Humane Society of Missouri has put chips in 7,500 newly adopted pets. The $25 procedure is mandatory and is included in the $62 adoption fee for a dog and the $57 fee for a cat.

The chip can be put into any pet, including birds and turtles. Although tattoos and tags are more easily seen, the chip links more information to the animal and cannot

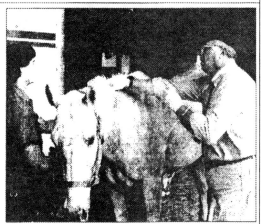

Renyold Ferguson/Post-Dispatch

ABOVE: Queeny Park ranger Cheryl Fechter holds Cutter, one of the rangers' horses, at the park stables on Friday while Dr. Chris Rolf inserts an identity microchip into the horse's neck.

ABOVE: The microchip (bottom left) as compared to a dime and a band pole of a wrist watch. Also pictured is the syringe and needle used to insert the microchip. RIGHT: An instrument that reads the information on a microchip in a horse's neck.

fall off.

And that's good for the rangers' horses, whose jobs include working at parades, traffic control and public relations for the rangers, Wilson said.

"They look a lot friendlier than driving around in a police car," he said. "No one wants to pet a police car."

for dogs and other animals. Even Queen Elizabeth II's dog has a chip. Other animals that have been microchipped include cattle, turtles, birds, snakes, and even fish. A hand-held external scanner uses radio signals to find the encoded ID number in the microchipped animals.

Once the microchips had successfully helped to locate lost pets, stopped many poachers, tracked migratory habits of wildlife, and even detected the number of endangered species, the public was primed. The next step: microchip implants in humans. Once again it all started so innocently. In the early 1990s, participants in sport-

San Francisco Chronicle

NORTHERN CALIFORNIA'S LARGEST NEWSPAPER

THURSDAY, APRIL 27, 1995

Novato Orders Microchip IDs for Cats

Implants would be between shoulders

By Tyro Mead
Chronicle North Bay Bureau

Overriding objections that their actions had Orwellian overtones, Novato City Council members mandated early yesterday that all cats have identifying microchips implanted between their shoulder blades.

In addition, the council's new cat-licensing law decrees that every cat that spends any time out of doors and is 4 months or older must be sterilized.

"If people did not permit their cats to breed, if animals weren't dying by the millions in shelters across the United States, we wouldn't need this ordinance," said Diane Allevato, executive director of the Marin Humane Society and sponsor of the law. "This ordinance makes social policy ... There comes a point when the social ethic of a community has to reflect the rights of animals."

Allevato said even though the vast majority of cats who wind up at the society's shelter are clearly someone's pet, only 14 percent are ever claimed. In contrast, dogs — which have been licensed for years — are reunited with their owners 80 percent of time.

She said the cat ordinance is intended to raise the reunion rate and lower the cat population. Allevato said her agency had to euthanize more than 1,000 cats last year.

Since the society began a voluntary microchip identification

CATS: Page A13 Col 1

CATS: Implants Ordered

From Page 1

program six years ago, Allevato said, the reunion rate has shot up by 200 percent.

But during a lengthy city council session that ran into the early morning hours yesterday, some opponents suggested that the price outweighed the potential benefits.

"It's a futuristic, George Orwellian attitude toward animals," said Pascale Weimerskirch of Sausalito, who said he feared that other Marin cities would follow Novato's lead.

Other opponents argued passionately that cat-licensing laws, however well-intentioned, can actually lead to more animals being abandoned.

"I think it's an inappropriate extension of government bureaucracy," said Nathan Winograd, a spokesman for the California Humane Coalition, an umbrella organization for 50 animal-care groups around the state. "Responsible people will take care of their cats. Irresponsible people won't."

The opponents also expressed concern that the measure would hurt feral cats and the people who care for them.

"I'm not sure I want to see a discrimination against the cats that don't have so-called owners," said Elliot Katz, a veterinarian and the founder of San Rafael-based In Defense of Animals. If a home cannot be found for a healthy, sterilized cat, he argued, then it should be returned to where it was found instead of being euthanized.

With the measure, Novato joins a number of Bay Area cities — including San Jose, which also passed a licensing measure yesterday

which have adopted the attitude that cat owners should be treated like dog owners and be required to register their pets. Most do not have a sterilization requirement, however, and the microchip mandate is a novel twist to Novato's measure.

In the measure's original version, each cat would have been required to have a microchip — a rice-sized pellet that has been encoded with information about the human responsible for the animal — injected into the ruff of its neck. But at the tail end of Tuesday's council session, Mayor Bernard Meyers pressed for an amendment that allows anyone who takes a strong exception to the microchip plan to opt for a more expensive collar and tag.

The annual $7 license fee will include the cost of the microchip the first time it is issued. A collar-and-tag license will cost $15. Spaying and neutering surgeries run from $25 to $50.

The Humane Society will be responsible for coordinating the measure's implementation. The ordinance specifies that the Humane Society will provide low-cost or free spay-neuter surgery to any pet whose owner cannot afford to pay. It also calls for $45 fines.

Residents whose animals are not licensed will be given a "fix-it" ticket and have 20 days to comply. No one speaking in favor of the measure apologized for the pun.

The measure passed 3 to 1 and will take effect in six months. Councilman Dennis Fishwick, who had wanted an amendment stating that no cat would be euthanized as a result of the ordinance, was the single vote against.

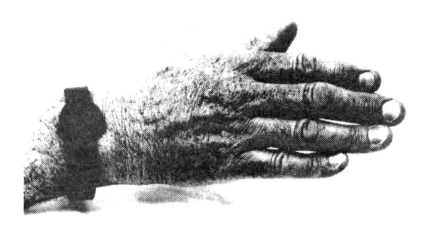

Bracelet transponder

ing events such as runners, swimmers, and skiers wore velcro brace-
lets with transponders.[130]

By the mid-'90s, the microchip implant crowd came out of the
closet. An article from *Popular Science* of July 1995 states: "If we
had our way, we'd implant a chip behind everyone's ear in the ma-
ternity ward." The prestigious *Forbes Magazine* of September 22,
1997, entitles an article "No Place to Hide." (Recall the very same
statement by Senator Frank Church.)

> The typical American family in 2008: Above their home, foot-long
> robot airplanes patrol several hundred feet up, on the lookout for
> criminals and even casual pot smokers. Both family cars are
> equipped with global-positioning satellite receivers and locator
> beacons. Mom and Dad carry cell phones that double as personal
> locators that can find them anywhere on the planet. The parents,
> the kids, and the dogs, all have microchips under their skin with
> ID.

The top headline to this article states: "Get ready for the surveillance society. It will make things tougher for killers, rapists, cheat-
ing husbands, and bad guys in general. It will also be very conve-

nient for potential dictators." Once again, this article sounds like a paraphrase of Revelation chapter thirteen.

In the April 27, 1998, edition of *Time* magazine, was an article entitled "The Future of Money." In the future, your cash, your credit cards, your ATM card, your ID card, your insurance card, and your life will be on one card or chip. The article goes on to say: "Your daughter can store the money any way she wants — on her laptop, on a debit card, even (in the not-too-distant future) on a chip implanted under her skin."

Another article in *Time* magazine dated August 9, 1999, tells the story of two babies who were switched at birth in the state-owned University of Maryland Medical Center. After this happened the medical center began to implant electronic belly-button chips on newborns. This could set a legal precedent for all state-owned medical centers across America. Very soon microchip implants will be used worldwide — from the "cradle to the grave."

The world's newest microchip or digital transceiver implant for humans is the "Digital Angel,"[131] created by Applied Digital Solutions. The patent rights have already been acquired. The Digital Angel will be implanted just under the skin with maintenance-free regenerating powers, supplied electromechanically, through the movement of muscles. One of the main purposes of Digital Angel is to track and locate lost or missing individuals by global positioning satellites. Interestingly, the implant will also be used for law enforcement, e-business security, and medical monitoring.

Richard J. Sullivan, chairman and CEO of Applied Digital Solutions, said "the Digital Angel's multipurpose technology would enable them to tap into a vast global market with an estimated total value in excess of one hundred billion dollars."[132] For Christians, it is plain to see in light of the Holy Scriptures where all of these high-tech implants are leading. We need to remember that not every person or member of any of the organizations we have discussed has been plotting to take over the world by having everyone take a microchip implant, for they have not. Many of these people are well-meaning, law-abiding citizens who really believe their ideas and so-phisticated technology will greatly enhance society, not enslave it.

For people who do not believe the Holy Scriptures, who look at this technology from a human perspective, the imbedding of micro-chips beneath the skin offers many good possibilities and benefits. Just think! No more waiting in lines for the rest of your life, never showing an ID, buying a ticket, carrying keys or a wallet, remem-bering a password or PIN number. Family and friends could find you instantly in any crowd. Imagine just putting out your hand and watching lights snap on, doors automatically opening, and money popping out of an ATM. According to some, microchip implants un-der the skin would create a crime-free society. No more cash robber-ies, stolen credit cards, or kidnapping. Anyone wanting access to a gun could only be allowed to do so if he had one of these implants. If a person tried to enter a school building, church, or work place where he should not be, the building's computer would deny access. No more Columbine, Paducah, or Jonesboro shootings. No more church shootings or work place shootings. Probably the greatest benefit of the microchip implant would be to track, identify, and locate every person's whereabouts in the world at all times. What could ever go wrong with all of this freedom, security, safety, and convenience by simply placing a small chip under your skin? Sounds like a New World Order Utopia and paradise to the casual observer. *That is,* until the world dictator comes on the scene and uses this technology for evil instead of good. On the authority of God's Word, the world dictator will come!

The most sobering and dramatic example of an individual re-ceiving a surgically-implanted microchip is Kevin Warwick, the world-renowned professor of cybernetics at the world-renowned University of Reading in the U.K. We quote from the August 26, 1998, edition of the *Daily Telegraph,* page 3:

> As he walks through his front door, the lights click on automati-cally, the music swells, the bath fills to a perfect temperature, and

the wine knows to chill itself. It is the end of another ordinary day as Mr. Cyborg — half husband, half machine — comes home. . . . Prof. Kevin Warwick has become the first person to have a silicon chip implanted in his body. "The chip allows computers to communicate directly with my body," he said. "As I walk around the building, lights go on and computers burst into life every time I scratch my head." Prof. Warwick's experiment is the first to link machines and mankind in a Faustian pact that could see us controlling our environment simply by our thoughts and movements — or, if it all goes wrong, giving machines the ability to control every aspect of our lives. "Man and machines have always worked separately. Today, for the first time, we have united to make a better world," Prof. Warwick said. . . . Liz Lucas, his secretary, can find the professor's whereabouts simply by looking at a computer screen. . . . "Since the implant, we always know where he is," she said. *The ultimate application* is to *tap into the brain's thought processes* — an area that is currently a mystery to scientists. "Instead of having the memory and thought processing capacity of your brain, you could have the capabilities of an extremely powerful computer."

Believe it or not, scientists working for British Telecom are currently developing a new microchip for implantation in the skull, just behind the eye. It will record a person's every thought, experience, and sensation. Hence its name: Soul Catcher 2025.[133] Dr. Chris Winter, of British Telecom's Artificial Life Team, stated: "This is the end of death. By combining people's lives on a computer with a record of a person's genes, we could recreate a person physically, emotionally, and spiritually."[134] They could not have picked a better name for the microchip implant than Soul Catcher.

Now that scientists believe they can "end death" and "recreate a person . . . spiritually," it is clear to see they have fallen prey to Satan's ultimate lie in the Garden of Eden, "ye shall be as gods."

Just as Eve was deceived in the beginning, mankind is being

deceived in the end-times. Could this lie, "ye shall be as gods," and the implanting of the Soul Catcher microchip be the "strong delusion" that God will send mankind?

One thing is certain, when a person receives the mark of the Beast in their hand or in their forehead to buy, sell, and worship the Beast and his image "he shall be tormented with fire and brimstone . . . And the smoke of their torment ascendeth up for ever and ever and they have no rest day nor night" (Rev. 14:10–11). On the other hand, if a person refuses to take the mark of the Beast, they will be beheaded according to Revealtion 20:4.

Recently there was legislation passed that could possibly be the foundation for decapitation. On March 26, 1991, H. J. Resolution 104 was signed into law. Also the joint resolution of the House and

---

105 STAT. 44   PUBLIC LAW 102-14—MAR. 20, 1991

Public Law 102-14
102d Congress

Joint Resolution

Mar. 20, 1991
[H.J. Res. 104]

To designate March 26, 1991, as "Education Day, U.S.A.".

Whereas Congress recognizes the historical tradition of ethical values and principles which are the basis of civilized society and upon which our great Nation was founded;

Whereas these ethical values and principles have been the bedrock of society from the dawn of civilization, when they were known as the Seven Noahide Laws;

Whereas without these ethical values and principles the edifice of civilization stands in serious peril of returning to chaos;

Whereas society is profoundly concerned with the recent weakening of these principles that has resulted in crises that beleaguer and threaten the fabric of civilized society;

Whereas the justified preoccupation with these crises must not let the citizens of this Nation lose sight of their responsibility to transmit these historical ethical values from our distinguished past to the generations of the future;

Whereas the Lubavitch movement has fostered and promoted these ethical values and principles throughout the world;

Whereas Rabbi Menachem Mendel Schneerson, leader of the Lubavitch movement, is universally respected and revered and his eighty-ninth birthday falls on March 26, 1991;

Whereas in tribute to this great spiritual leader, "the rebbe", this, his ninetieth year will be seen as one of "education and giving", the year in which we turn to education and charity to return the world to the moral and ethical values contained in the Seven Noahide Laws; and

Whereas this will be reflected in an international scroll of honor signed by the President of the United States and other heads of state: Now, therefore, be it

Resolved by the Senate and House of Representatives of the United States of America in Congress assembled, That March 26,

Senate established Public Law No. 102-14 and designated March 26, 1991, as "Education Day, U.S.A." On March 20, 1991, former President George Bush approved this joint resolution.

This law was allegedly to honor Rabbi Menachem Scheerson, a great spiritual leader, on his ninetieth birthday. Written into all the "Whereas's" were incorporated two references calling for the return to the ethical values of the "Seven Noahide Laws." As we make a cursory examination of the laws, we do not see anything blatantly objectionable. Neither will you find any call for decapitation in this harmless appearing document, but beware, there is much more than meets the eye.

When you dig into the historical documents of the ancient Jewish Talmud with reference to the Noahide Laws, guess what you will find . . . "decapitation" for breaking certain commandments.

Before we go any further, our government *did not* call for the establishment of capital punishment by decapitation in Public Law No. 102-14, but I believe the foundation for such a law has been laid.

The Noahide Laws are defined in the *Jewish Encyclopedia,* KTAV Publishing House, Inc., pages 648–649, followed by the prescribed punishment:

LAWS, NOACHIAN:
(1) not to worship idols; (2) not to blaspheme the name of God; (3) to establish courts of justice; (4) not to kill; (5) not to commit adultery; and (6) not to rob. . . .

. . . The prevalent opinion in the Talmud is that there are only seven laws which are binding upon all mankind. . . .

In the elaboration of these seven Noachian laws, and in assigning punishments for their transgression, the Rabbis are sometime more lenient and sometimes more rigorous with Noachidae [non-Jews] than with Israelites. With but a few exceptions, the punishment meted out to a Noachid for the transgression of any of the seven laws is **decapitation**, the least painful of the four

modes of execution of criminals. The many formalities of procedures essential when the accused is an Israelite *need not be observed in the case of the Noachid.* The latter may be convincted on
the testimony of one *witness,* even on that of relatives, but not on
that of a woman. He need have had no warning from the witnesses; and a *single judge* may pass sentence on him. . . .

Under the Noahide laws during the Tribulation period, Christians
could be considered guilty of violating the blasphemy law. Christians believe that Jesus, the Christ, is God in the flesh (John 1:1,
14). Recall that Antichrist will "sit in the temple of God, shewing
himself that he is God" (2 Thess. 2:4). If a Christian will not worship the Antichrist, they could be found guilty of blasphemy.

In the July-August issue of *The Gap* newsletter, published by
the Noahide movement, the lead article revealed that there is pres-
sure being applied for *worldwide* recognition of the seven Noahide
Laws. Professor of International Law Ernest Easterly, Southern University Law Center, said: "With further recognition by other nations and international courts, the Seven Noahide Laws should become the cornerstone of a truly civilized international legal order."

Welcome to the New World Order! The following information is
about legislation that was put before the state of Georgia proposing
execution by the guillotine. The legislation is being offered as an
alternative option for convicts sentenced to the death penalty.

Guillotine Proposed as Means of Execution in Georgia

Georgia lawmaker Doug Teper (Democrat, 61st Dist.) has proposed
a bill to replace the state's electric chair with the guillotine. Teper's reasoning? It would allow for death-row inmates as organ do-
nors, he said, since the "blade makes a clean cut and leaves vital
organs intact. . . ."

The guillotine, invented by the French Dr. Guillotine, was
mainly used in the 18th and 19th century and chops off a person's
head. It hasn't been used for decades in any country in the world.

Excerpts from Georgia's legislation H.B. No. 1274 follow:

Be It Enacted by the General Assembly of Georgia:

SECTION 1: The General Assembly finds that while prisoners condemned to death may wish to donate one or more of their organs for transplant, any such desire is thwarted by the fact that electrocution makes all such organs unsuitable for transplant. The intent of the General Assembly in enacting this legislation is to provide for a method of execution which is compatible with the donation of organs by a condemned prisoner.

SECTION 2(a): All persons who have been convicted of a capital offense and have imposed upon them a sentence of death shall, at the election of the condemned, suffer such punishment either by electrocution or by guillotine. If the condemned fails to make an election by the thirtieth day preceding the date scheduled for execution, punishment shall be by electrocution.

SECTION 3: The Department of Corrections shall provide a death chamber and all necessary apparatus, machinery, and appliances for inflicting the penalty of death by electrocution or by guillotine.

SECTION 4: This Act shall be applicable to all executions occurring on or after August 31, 1996.

The Georgia legislation for beheading by means of a guillotine failed to pass. But, rest assured, the "nuts and bolts" are in place and you have not heard or seen the last of such attempts . . . the Bible says so in Revelation.

Chapter 6

Invitation—How to Be Saved

I would like to ask you some personal questions about your relationship with Jesus Christ, the Son of God. If you are a Christian, maybe God is speaking to your heart right now about witnessing to your loved ones, friends, co-workers, or neighbors. Pray about giving them my video to watch or this book to read. As Christians, we know the best is yet to come because we have read the last few chapters of God's Word. Be a good Christian soldier, stay in the battle, put on the whole armor of God, put your hand to the plow, and don't look back. Let's win as many souls as we can for the glory of God. He that winneth souls is wise.

Maybe you are not sure if you *are* a Christian, or maybe you know that you *are not* a Christian. If Jesus were to come back today, do you know for sure He would take you back to heaven? Or, would you be left behind to go through the terrible seven-year Tribulation period and the New World Order? What will you do if the world police knock on your family's door and state: "Only individuals who receive the mark of the Beast will be permitted to buy or sell"? Remember, once you receive the mark of the Beast in your right hand or forehead, you have damned your soul to the lake of fire. This is the second death.

What if you died today? Where would you spend eternity? In heaven or hell?

The only way to have your sins forgiven and have everlasting life with the assurance of heaven, is by receiving God's gift of eternal life. That's correct. Eternal life is a *free gift* to everyone. God wants to give you that *free gift* of eternal life right now, but you must first admit to God you have sinned against Him. The penalty for sin is separation from God *forever* in the lake of fire, which is the second death.

God is not willing that any should perish, and to prove it He sent His only begotten Son, Jesus Christ, who died on the cross for your sin and mine. Please, I beg you right now, get on your knees and tell God in your own words that you have sinned against Him. You do believe Jesus died, was buried, and rose again. Tell Him you want the gift of eternal life, *Jesus Christ.* I trust you will settle your eternal destiny because, "now is the accepted time, behold, now is the day of salvation."

Thank you, and God bless!

End Notes

1. A Constitution for the Federation of Earth, World Constitution and Parliament Association, 8800 W. 14th Ave., Lakewood, Colorado.
2. Terry Cook, *The Mark of the New World Order,* p. 9, Virtue International Publishing, Indianapolis, Indiana.
3. Rob Lindsted, Ph.D., *Can You Really Know Your Future?,* p. 53, Bible Truth, Wichita, Kansas.
4. Professional audiotapes recorded live at State of the World Forum by Sound True Recordings, Boulder, Colorado.
5. *www.earthcharter.org*
6. *www.gci.ch/Green Cross Family/gorby/gorby.html*
7. Mikhail Gorbachev, "The Earth Charter," Speech: Rio+5 Forum, March 18, 1997.
8. Gorbachev, "Environment: Act Globally, Not Nationally," Interview with the *Los Angeles Times.*
9. Samantha Smith, journalist, testimony of her observations at the State of the World Forum, San Francisco, September 27–October 1, 1995.
10. Smith, "Gorbachev Forum Highlights World Government," *Hope for the World Update,* p. 2.
11. World Constitution and Parliament Association, 8800 West 14th Ave., Lakewood, Colorado 80215, *www.wcpagren.org.*
12. Ibid.
13. Gary Kah, *The New World Religion,* p. 167, Hope International Publishing, Noblesville, Indiana.
14. Ibid., pp. 84–85.
15. *www.whitehouse.com*
16. Beverly LaHaye, Concerned Women for America newsletter, July 1999, p. 2, Washington, D.C.
17. Don McAlvany, *Storm Warning,* p. 133, Hearthstone Publishing, Oklahoma City, Oklahoma.
18. Ibid., pp. 184–190.
19. David Barton, *Original Intent,* p. 110, Wall Builders, Aledo, Texas.
20. Rexford G. Tugwell, *Harper and Row,* 1974, Liberty Library, Washington, D.C.

21. Newstates of America Constitution, p. 1
22. Joan Veon, *The United Nations Global Straitjacket,* p. 85, Hearthstone Publishing, Oklahoma City, Oklahoma.
23. Joan Collins, *Constitution in Crisis,* pp. 36–37, Hearthstone Publishing, Oklahoma City, Oklahoma.
24. McAlvany, *Storm Warning,* p. 195.
25. Ibid., pp. 149–150.
26. *Your United Nations: Official Guidebook,* introduction.
27. Ibid., p. 1.
28. Ibid., p. 1.
29. Ibid., introduction.
30. *Newsweek,* September 29, 1997, cover.
31. Veon, *Global Straitjacket,* p. 105.
32. Ibid., p. 106.
33. *Global Biodiversity Assessment,* p. 534, published for the United Nations Environment Programme, Cambridge University Press, 1995.
34. Map of "The U.S. Man and the Biosphere Program," produced by Environmental Perspectives Inc., Bangor, Maine, 1998. Special thanks to Chris Hunter for driving eight thousand miles across America to take pictures of UNESCO signs in Biosphere Reserves and World Heritage Sites. Also, special thanks to Betty Sukuma for her pictures of World Heritage Sites.
35. Dr. Cathy Burns, *Masonic and Occult Symbols Illustrated,* p. 328, Sharint, Mount Carmel, Pennsylvania.
36. Ibid.
37. Ibid.
38. Ibid., p. 329.
39. National Park Service flyer, U.S. Department of the Interior, International Council on Monuments and Sites (US/ICOMOS), 1997.
40. Map of "The U.S. Man and Biosphere Program" produced by Dr. Michael Coffman of "Environmental Perspectives Inc.," Bangor, Maine, 1998.
41. Don McAlvany, *The McAlvany Intelligence Advisor,* p. 16, October 1997, Phoenix, Arizona.
42. *The New American,* August 18, 1997, p. 15.
43. Ibid., p. 16.
44. Ibid., p. 16.
45. Ibid., p. 16.
46. *Global Biodiversity Assessment,* Cambridge Univeristy Press, published for the United Nations Environment Programme, V. H. Heywood, executive editor, 1995.
47. *The New American,* August 18, 1997, p. 17, article by Dr. Michael Coffman, Ph.D., of Environmental Perspectives, Inc..

48. Ibid., p. 17.
49. *Global Biodiversity Assessment,* p. 993.
50. *The McAlvany Intelligence Advisor,* October 1997, p. 9.
51. *The New American,* August 18, 1997, p. 12, article by Dr. Michael Coffman.
52. Ibid.
53. Ibid.
54. Dr. Michael Coffman, 1229 Broadway, Suite 313, Bangor, Maine 04401. Phone 207/945-9878. Maps can be purchased.
55. *The New American,* August 18, 1997, p. 13, article by Dr. Michael Coffman.
56. Joan Veon, *The United Nations and Its Global Agenda for the Environment, Economy and Family,* chapter 3.
57. *The New American,* August 18, 1997, article by Dr. Michael Coffman.
58. *Thurmont Times Monthly,* July 1997, "In My Opinion" by Mike Dwyer, p. 5.
59. William T. James, *Fore Warning,* p. 285, Harvest House Publishers, Eugene, Oregon 97402.
60. *Global Biodiversity Assessment,* p. 839.
61. Ibid., p. 839.
62. The infamous "groves" are listed twenty-three times in the Old Testament. A few include Exodus 34:13; Deuteronomy 12:3; Judges 3:7; First Kings 18:19; Second Chronicles 33:3; and Isaiah 17:8.
63. *Global Biodiversity Assessment,* p. 839.
64. Ibid., pp. 337, 350–351, 728, 730, 738, 749, 755, 757, 771, 774, 782, and 970.
65. Ibid., p. 773.
66. Stanley Monteith, M.D., *The Population Control Agenda,* p. 6, Soquel, California, *www.industries.net/radio_liberty.*
67. Ibid., p. 5.
68. Ibid., p. 1.
69. William T. James, *Fore Warning,* p. 76.
70. Ibid., p. 78.
71. Ibid., p. 79.
72. Veon, *The United Nations Global Straitjacket,* p. 107.
73. Ibid., p. 112.
74. *Washington Post,* September 20, 1992, A27.
75. *Human Events,* November 3, 1995, p. 7, article by Cliff Kincaid.
76. Department of State Publication 7277, Disarmament Series 5, released September 1961, Bureau of Public Affairs, U.S. Government Printing Office.
77. *www.mikenew.com.*

78. Jews for the Preservation of Firearms Ownership, Inc., P.O. Box 270143, Hartford, Wisconsin 53027   *www.jpfo.org.*
79. Gary Kah, *Hope for the World Update,* pp. 3–4.
80. Ibid., p. 4.
81. Robert Muller, *New Genesis, Shaping a Global Spirituality,* p. 127, World Happiness and Cooperation, Anacortes, Washington.
82. Ibid.
83. Robert Keith Spenser, *United Nations Meditation Room,* p. 7, Emissary Publications, Clacakamas, Oregon, 1964.
84. Ibid., p. 8.
85. Ibid., p. 9.
86. G. A. Riplinger, *New Age Bible Versions,* p. 459, A. V. Publications, Munroe Falls, Ohio.
87. H. P. Blavatsky, *Lucifer Magazine, The Theosophical Publication,* Adelphi W. C. London, The Occult Publishing Co., Boston, Massachusetts, 1895.
88. Ibid., Vol. XVI, No. 93.
89. Gary Kah, *The New World Religion,* p. 24, 1998.
90. Ibid., p. 41.
91. Ibid., p. 25.
92. Ibid., p. 30.
93. Ibid., p. 31.
94. Ibid., p. 30.
95. Lucis Trust Newsletter, July 1995.
96. Dr. Dennis Cuddy, Ph.D., *Secret Records Revealed,* p. 200, Hearthstone Publishing, Oklahoma City, Oklahoma.
97. World Goodwill Newsletter, 1999, No. 2.   *www.lucistrust.org.*
98. G. A. Riplinger, *New Age Bible Versions,* p. 461.
99. Gary Kah, *The New World Religion,* p. 209.
100. Ibid., pp. 212–215.
101. United Religions Initiative 2000 flyer, 1055 Taylor St., San Francisco, California.   Telephone 415/440-2303. *www.unitedreligions.org.*
102. Ibid.
103. Robert Muller, *New Genesis,* p. XIII.
104. United Religions Initiative 2000 flyer.
105. Gary Kah, *Hope for the World Update,* Fall 1999, p. 5, article by Berit Kjos.
106. *World Scripture,* International Religious Foundation, Paragon House, Minnesota, 1995.
107. *www.worthynews.com.*   *www.pokemon.com.*
108. *www.crossroad.to.*
109. Gary Kah, *En Route to Global Occupation,* p. 42.

110. *www.europarl.eu.int.*
111. Dr. Jack Van Impe, *The '80s, the Antichrist and Your Startling Future,* p. 17, Royal Oak, Michigan.
112. *Forbes Magazine,* February 22, 1999, "Blue Mountain."
113. Ibid.
114. *gunter@interactive.net,* Terry Cook, *Big Brother NSA.*, S.C.M., Bend, Oregon.
115. Terry Cook, *Big Brother NSA,* pp. 20, 98, 100. *www.nsa.gov.8080.*
116. James Bamford, *The Puzzle Palace,* pp. 133–137, Penguin Books, New York, New York.
117. Ibid., p. 138.
118. *www.biometrics.org.*
119. James Bamford, *The Puzzle Palace,* pp. 378, 477.
120. *www.cbnnow.com* newsstand stories February 15, 2000.
121. Ibid.
122. *Automatic ID News,* August 1994, p. 20.
123. Ibid.
124. "Human Services" by Brian Miller, Sacramento County Department of Human Services, California.
125. *Automatic ID News,* Volume 11, Number 8, pp. 1, 18.
126. Terry Cook, *The Mark of the New World Order,* p. 518.
127. Ibid., p. 521.
128. Ibid., p. 628.
129. Ibid., p. 626.
130. Ibid., p. 331.
131. *www.applieddig.com*
132. Ibid.
133. Project Freedom, Truth Campaign *www.isleofavalon.co.uk/local/h-pages/pro-freedom/the beast.html*
134. Ibid.

Part II

Documents of
the New World Order

Project Megiddo

The attached analysis, entitled Project Megiddo, is an FBI strategic assessment of the potential for domestic terrorism in the United States undertaken in anticipation of or response to the arrival of the new millennium.

For over four thousand years, Megiddo, a hill in northern Israel, has been the site of many battles. Ancient cities were established there to serve as a fortress on the plain of Jezreel to guard a mountain pass. As Megiddo was built and rebuilt, one city upon the other, a mount or hill was formed. The Hebrew word "Armageddon" means "hill of Megiddo." In English, the word has come to represent battle itself. The last book of the New Testament of the Bible designates Armageddon as the assembly point in the apocalyptic setting of God's final and conclusive battle against evil. The name "Megiddo" is an apt title for a project that analyzes those who believe the year 2000 will usher in the end of the world and those who are willing to perpetrate acts of violence to bring that end about.

I. EXECUTIVE SUMMARY

The year 2000 is being discussed and debated at all levels of society. Most of the discussions regarding this issue revolve around the topic of technology and our society's overwhelming dependence on the multitude of computers and computer chips which make our world run smoothly. However, the upcoming millennium also holds important implications beyond the issue of computer technology. Many extremist individuals and groups place some significance on the next millennium, and as such it will present challenges by law enforcement at many levels. The significance is based primarily upon either religious beliefs relating to the Apocalypse or political beliefs relating to the New World Order (NWO) conspiracy theory. The challenge is how well law enforcement will prepare and respond.

The following report, entitled "Project Megiddo," is intended to analyze the potential for extremist criminal activity in the United States by individuals or domestic extremist groups who profess an apocalyptic view of the millennium or attach special significance to the year 2000. The purpose behind this assessment is to provide law enforcement agencies with a clear picture of potential extremism motivated by the next millennium. The report does not contain information on domestic terrorist groups whose actions are not influenced by the year 2000.

There are numerous difficulties involved in providing a thorough analysis of domestic security threats catalyzed by the new millennium. Quite simply, the very nature of the current domestic terrorism threat places severe limitations on effective intelligence gathering and evaluation. Ideological and philosophical belief systems which attach importance, and possibly violence, to the millennium have been well-articulated. From a law enforcement perspective, the problem therefore is not a lack of understanding of motivating ideologies: The fundamental problem is that the traditional focal point for counterterrorism analysis — the terrorist group — is not always well-defined or relevant in the current environment.

The general trend in domestic terrorism is the terrorist's disavowal of traditional, hierarchical, and structured terrorist organizations. Even well-established militias, which tend to organize along military lines with central control, are characterized by factionalism and disunity. While several "professional" terrorist groups still exist and present a continued threat to domestic security, the overwhelming majority of extremist groups in the United States have adopted a fragmented, leaderless structure where individuals or small groups act with autonomy. Clearly, the worst act of domestic terrorism in United States history was perpetrated by merely two individuals: Timothy McVeigh and Terry Nichols. In many cases, extremists of this sort are extremely difficult to identify until after an incident has occurred. Thus, analysis of domestic extremism in which the group serves as the focal point of evaluation has obvious limitations.

The Project Megiddo intelligence initiative has identified very few indications of specific threats to domestic security. Given the present nature of domestic extremism, this is to be expected. However, this is a function of the limitations of the group-oriented model of counterterrorism analysis and should not be taken necessarily as reflective of a minor or trivial domestic threat. Without question, this initiative has revealed indicators of potential violent activity on the part of extremists in this country. Militias, adherents of racist belief systems such as Christian Identity and Odinism, and other radical domestic extremists are clearly focusing on the millennium as a time of action. Certain individuals from these various perspectives are acquiring weapons, storing food and clothing, raising funds through fraudulent means, procuring safe houses, preparing compounds, surveying potential targets, and recruiting new converts. These and other indicators are not taking place in a vacuum, nor are they random or arbitrary. In the final analysis, while making specific predictions is extremely difficult, acts of violence in commemoration of the millennium are just as likely to occur as not. In the absence of intelligence that the more established and organized terrorist groups are planning millennial violence as an organizational strategy, violence is most likely to be perpetrated by radical fringe members of established groups. For example, while Aryan Nations leader Richard Butler publicly frowns on proactive violence, adherents of his religion or individual members of his organization may commit acts of violence autonomously.

Potential cult-related violence presents additional challenges to law enforcement. The potential for violence on behalf of members of biblically-driven cults is determined almost exclusively by the whims of the cult leader. Therefore, effective intelligence and analysis of such cults requires an extensive understanding of the cult leader. Cult members generally act to serve and please the cult leader rather than accomplish an ideological objective. Almost universally, cult leaders are viewed as messianic in the eyes of their followers. Also, the cult leader's prophecies, preachings, orders, and objectives are subject to indiscriminate change. Thus, while analysis of publicly stated goals and objectives of cults may provide hints of their behavior and intentions, it is just as likely to be uninformed or, at worst, misleading. Much more valuable is a thorough examination of the cult leader, his position of power over his followers, and an awareness of the responding behavior and activity of the cult. Sudden changes in activity — for example, less time spent on "Bible study" and more time spent on "physical training" — indicate that the cult may be preparing for some type of action.

The millennium holds special signicance for many, and as this pivotal point in time approaches, the impetus for the initiation of violence becomes more acute. Several religiously motivated groups envision a quick, fiery ending in an apocalyptic battle. Others may initiate a sustained campaign of terrorism in the United States to prevent the NWO. Armed with the urgency of the millennium as a motivating factor, new clandestine groups may conceivably form to engage in violence toward the U.S. Government or its citizens.

Most importantly, this analysis clearly shows that perceptions matter. The perceptions of the leaders and followers of extremist organizations will contribute much toward the ultimate course of action they choose. For example, in-depth analysis of Y2K compliancy on the part of various key sectors that rely on computers has determined that, despite a generally positive outlook for overall compliance, there will be problem industries and minor difficulties and inconveniences.[1] If they occur, these inconveniences are likely to cause varying responses by the extreme fringes. Members of various groups, for example, have identified potentially massive power failures as an indication of a United Nations-directed NWO takeover. While experts have indicated that only minor brownouts will occur, various militias are likely to *perceive* such minor brownouts as indicative of a larger conspiracy.[2]

The Senate Special Committee on the Year 2000 Technology Problem has stated that some state and local governments could be unprepared, including the inability to provide benefit payments.[3] This could have a significant impact on major urban areas, resulting in the possibility for civil unrest. Violent white supremacists are likely to view such unrest as an affirmation of a racist, hate-filled world view. Likewise, militia members who predict the implementation of martial law in response to a Y2K computer failure would become all the more fearful.

II. INTRODUCTION

Are we already living on the precipice of the Apocalypse — the chaotic final period of warfare between the forces of good and evil signaling the second coming of Christ, as forecast in the New Testament's Book of Revelation? Or, will life on earth continue for another 1,000 years, allowing humans to eliminate disease and solve the mysteries of the aging process so they can live as long as Methuselah, colonize space, commune with extraterrestrials, unravel the secrets of teleportation, and usher in a golden age of peace and productivity?[4]

---

1. U.S. Congress, Senate, Special Committee on the Year 2000 Technology Problem, *Investigating the Impact of the Year 2000 Problem,* February 24, 1996, pp. 1–6.
2. Ibid., p. 3.
3. Ibid., p. 5
4. Cliff Linedecker, *Prophecies for the New Millennium* (Lantana, FL: Micromags, 1999), pp. 3–4.

At first glance, some of the predictions compiled in *Prophecies for the New Millennium* that claim to foretell how the millennium will affect the United States seem benign. In fact, those predictions capture some of the countless ways that domestic terrorists view how the millennium will affect the world. The threat posed by extremists as a result of perceived events associated with the Year 2000 (Y2K) is very real.

Numerous religious extremists claim that a race war will soon begin, and have taken steps to become martyrs in their predicted battle between good and evil. Three recent incidents committed by suspects who adhere to ideologies that emphasize millennial related violence illustrate those beliefs: Buford O. Furrow, Jr., the man charged in the August 1999 shootings at a Los Angeles area Jewish day care center, told authorities "it's time for America to wake and kill the Jews"; Ben Smith, who committed suicide after shooting at minorities in Indiana and Illinois, killing two and injuring ten, over the July 4, 1999, weekend, was found to have literature in his home that indicated the year 2000 would be the start of the killing of minorities; and John William King, the man convicted in the dragging death of James Byrd, Jr., a black man in Jasper, Texas, believed that his actions would help to initiate a race war. Each of these men believed in the imminence of a racial holy war.

Meanwhile, for members of the militia movement the new millennium has a political overtone rather than a religious one. It is their belief that the United Nations has created a secret plan, known as the New World Order (NWO), to conquer the world beginning in 2000. The NWO will be set in motion by the Y2K computer crisis.

Religious motivation and the NWO conspiracy theory are the two driving forces behind the potential for millennial violence. As the end of the millennium draws near, biblical prophecy and political philosophy may merge into acts of violence by the more extreme members of domestic terrorist groups that are motivated, in part, by religion. The volatile mix of apocalyptic religions and NWO conspiracy theories may produce violent acts aimed at precipitating the end of the world as prophesied in the Bible.

When and how Christ's second coming will occur is a critical point in the ideology of those motivated by extremist religious beliefs about the millennium. There is no consensus within Christianity regarding the specific date that the Apocalypse will occur. However, within many right-wing religious groups there is a uniform belief that the Apocalypse is approaching. Some of these same groups also point to a variety of non-religious indicators such as gun control, the Y2K computer problem, the NWO, the banking system, and a host of other "signs" that the Apocalypse is near. Almost uniformly, the belief among right-wing religious extremists is that the federal government is an arm of Satan. Therefore, the millennium will bring about a battle between Christian martyrs and the government. At the core of this volatile mix is the belief of apocalyptic religions and cults that the battle against Satan, as prophesied in the Book of Revelation, will begin in 2000.

An example of the confrontational nature and belief system of religiously motivated suspects illustrates the unique challenges that law enforcement faces when dealing with a fatalist/martyr philosophy. It also illustrates the domino effect that may occur after such a confrontation. Gordon Kahl, an adherent to the anti-government/racist Chrisian Identity religion, escaped after a 1983 shootout with police that left two Deputy U.S. Marshals dead. He was later killed during a subsequent shootout with the FBI and others that also left a county sheriff dead. In response to the killing of Kahl, Bob Mathews, a believer in the racist Odinist ideology, founded The Order. After The Order committed numerous crimes, its members were eventually tracked down. Mathews escaped after engaging in a gun battle and later wrote,

> Why are so many men so eager to destroy their own kind for the benefit of the Jews and the mongrels? I see three FBI agents hiding behind some trees. . . . I could have easily killed them. . . . They look like good racial stock yet all their talents are given to a gov-

ernment which is openly trying to mongrelize the very race these agents are part of. . . . I have been a good soldier, a fearless warrior. I will die with honor and join my brothers in [heaven].

Exemplifying his beliefs as a martyr, Mathews later burned to death in an armed standoff with the FBI.

In light of the enormous amount of millennial rhetoric, the FBI sought to analyze a number of variables that have the potential to spark violent acts perpetrated by domestic terrorists. Religious beliefs, the Y2K computer problem, and gun control laws all have the potential to become catalysts for such terrorism. The following elements are essential to understanding the phenomenon of domestic terrorism related to the millennium.

When Does the New Millenniun Begin?

As the nation and the world prepare to celebrate the arrival of the new millennium, a debate has arisen as to the correct date for its beginning. Although the true starting point of the next millennium is January 1, 2001, as established by the U.S. Naval Observatory in Washington, D.C., our nation's official time keeper, many will celebrate January 1, 2000, as the start of the millennium. The majority of domestic terrorists, like the general public, place a greater significance on January 1, 2000.

Blueprint for Action: The Turner Diaries

Many right-wing extremists are inspired by *The Turner Diaries,* a book written by William Pierce (under the pseudonym Andrew Macdonald), the leader of the white supremacist group National Alliance. The book details a violent overthrow of the federal government by white supremacists and also describes a brutal race war that is to take place simultaneously. To date, several groups or individuals have been inspired by this book:

- At the time of his arrest, Timothy McVeigh, the man responsible for the Oklahoma City bombing, had a copy of *The Turner*

Diaries in his possession. McVeigh's action against the Murrah Federal Building was strikingly similar to an event described in the book where the fictional terrorist group blows up FBI Headquarters.

- The Order, an early 1980s terrorist cell involved in murder, robberies, and counterfeiting, was motivated by the book's scenarios for a race war. The group murdered Alan Berg, a Jewish talk show host, and engaged in other acts of violence in order to hasten the race war described in the book. The Order's efforts later inspired another group, The New Order, which planned to commit similar crimes in an effort to start a race war that would lead to a national revolution.[5]

- Most recently, *The Turner Diaries* provided inspiration to John William King, the man convicted for dragging a black man to his death in Jasper, Texas. As King shackled James Byrd's legs to the back of his truck he was reported to say, "We're going to start *The Turner Diaries* early."[6]

During the year 2000 and beyond, *The Turner Diaries* will be an inspiration for right-wing terrorist groups to act because it outlines both a revolutionary takeover of the government and a race war. These elements of the book appeal to a majority of right-wing extremists because it is their belief that one or both events will coincide.

Interpretations of the Bible

Religiously based domestic terrorists use the New Testament's Book of Revelation — the prophecy of the endtime — for the foundation of their belief in the Apocalypse. Religious extremists interpret the symbolism portrayed in the Book of Revelation and mold it to pre-

---

5. Charles Bosworth, Jr., "Illinois Man Sought Start of Race War," *St. Louis Post-Dispatch,* March 15, 1998.
6. Paul Duggan, "From Beloved Son to Murder Suspect," *Washington Post,* February 16, 1999.

dict that the endtime is now and that the Apocalypse is near. To understand many religious extremists, it is crucial to know the origin of the Book of Revelation and the meanings of its words, numbers, and characters.

The Book of Revelation was written by a man named "John" who was exiled by the Roman government to a penal colony — the island of Patmos — because of his beliefs in Christ.[7] While on the island, he experienced a series of visions, described in the Book of Revelation. The writing in the Book of Revelation is addressed to churches who were at the time experiencing or were threatened by persecution from Rome because they were not following the government. For this reason, some believe the Book of Revelation was written in code language, much of which was taken from other parts of the Bible.

One interpretation describing the essence of the message contained in Revelation is that God will overcome Christianity's enemies (Roman government/Satan) and that the persecuted communities should persevere.[8] For right-wing groups who believe they are being persecuted by the satanic government of the United States, the Book of Revelation's message fits perfectly into their world view. This world view, in combination with a literal interpretation of the Book of Revelation, is reflected in extremist ideology, violent acts, and literature. For this reason, it is imperative to know the meaning of some of the "code words" frequently used:

- Four (4) signifies the world.
- Six (6) signifies imperfection.

---

7. While he never claimed to be the book's author, the Apostle John was identified as such by several of the early church Fathers. Authorship is generally ascribed to him today.

8. This interpretation of the Book of Revelation is according to the Catholic Bible and a Catholic scholar that was consulted on the matter. However, there are other varying interpretations of the Book of Revelation within Christianity.

- Seven (7) is the totality of perfection or fullness and completion.
- Twelve (12) represents the twelve tribes of Israel or the twelve apostles.
- One thousand (1,000) signifies immensity.
- The color white symbolizes power and can also represent victory, joy, and resurrection.
- The color red symbolizes a bloody war.
- The color black symbolizes famine.
- A rider on a pale green horse is a symbol of Death itself.
- "Babylon" is the satanic Roman government, now used to describe the U.S. government.[9]

Black Hebrew Israelites, a black supremacist group, typify the use of numerology from the Book of Revelation. They believe group members will comprise the 144,000 people who are saved by God in the second coming that is outlined in Revelation (7:1–17). In the Book of Revelation, John is shown a vision of 144,000 martyrs who have survived and did not submit to Satan. This number is derived from the assertion that the twelve tribes of Israel consisted of twelve thousand people each.

Groups not only use the Bible to interpret the endtimes, but use it to justify their ideology. Phineas Priests, an amorphous group of Christian Identity adherents, base their entire ideology on Chapter 25 of the Book of Numbers. The passage depicts a scene where Phineas kills an Israelite who was having relations with a Midianite woman and God then granted Phineas and all of his descendants a pledge of everlasting priesthood. Modern day followers of the Phineas Priest ideology believe themselves to be the linear descendants of Phineas and this passage gives them biblical justification to punish those who transgress God's laws. Therefore, the group is ardently opposed

---

9. All symbolism was taken from *The Catholic Bible: New American Bible.*

to race mixing and strongly believes in racial separation. The number 25 is often used as a symbol of the group.

Apocalyptic Religious Beliefs

To understand the mind set of why religious extremists would actively seek to engage in violent confrontations with law enforcement, the most common extremist ideologies must be understood. Under these ideologies, many extremists view themselves as religious martyrs who have a duty to initiate or take part in the coming battles against Satan. Domestic terrorist groups who place religious significance on the millennium believe the federal government will act as an arm of Satan in the final battle. By extension, the FBI is viewed as acting on Satan's behalf.

The philosophy behind targeting the federal government or entities perceived to be associated with it is succinctly described by Kerry Noble, a former right-wing extremist. He says the right-wing "envision[s] a dark and gloomy endtime scenario, where some Antichrist makes war against Christians."[10] The House of Yahweh, a Texas based religious group whose leaders are former members of the tax protesting Posse Comitatus, is typical: Hawkins (the leader) has interpreted biblical scripture that the Israeli Peace Accord signed on October 13, 1993, has started a seven-year period of tribulation which will end on October 14, 2000, with the return of Yeshua (the Messiah).[11] He also has interpreted that the FBI will be the downfall of the House of Yahweh and that the Waco Branch Davidian raids in 1993 were a warning to the House of Yahweh from the federal government, which he terms "the beast."[12] Similarly, Richard

---

10. Kerry Noble, *Tabernacle of Hate: Why They Bombed Oklahoma City* (Prescott, Ontario, Canada: Voyageur Publishing, 1998).
11. Robert Draper, "Happy Doomsday," *Texas Montly,* July 1997, p. 74; Evan Moore, "A House Divided: Tensions divide Abilene-area cult," *Houston Chronicle,* March 24, 1996.
12. Evan Moore, "A House Divided: Tensions divide Abilene-area cult," *Houston Chronicle,* March 24, 1996.

Butler, leader of the white supremacist group Aryan Nations, said the following when asked what might have motivated the day care shooting by Buford O. Furrow, Jr., one of his group's followers: "There's a war against the white race. There's a war of extermination against the white male."[13]

Unlike religiously based terrorists, militia anxiety and paranoia specifically relating to the year 2000 are based mainly on a political ideology. Some militia members read significance into 2000 as it relates to their conception of the NWO conspiracy.[14] The NWO conspiracy theory holds that the United Nations (U.N.) will lead a military coup against the nations of the world to form a socialist or One World Government. U.N. troops will mainly use foreign troops on American soil because foreigners will have fewer reservations about killing American citizens. U.S. armed forces will not attempt to stop this invasion by U.N. troops and, in fact, the U.S. military may be "deputized" as a branch of the U.N. armed forces. The American military contingent overseas will also play a large part in this elaborate conspiracy theory, as they will be used to help conquer the rest of the world. The rationale for this part of the theory is that American soldiers will also have less qualms about killing foreigners, as opposed to killing their own citizens.

Under this hypothetical NWO/One World Government, the following events are to take place: 1) private property rights and private gun ownership will be abolished; 2) all national, state, and local elections will become meaningless, since they will be controlled by the U.N.; 3) the U.S. Constitution will be supplanted by the U.N.

---

13. John K. Wiley, "Profile of attack suspect is familiar and frightening," *Miami Herald,* August 12, 1999.

14. Use of this term within militia circles became more common after President Bush started using it to refer to the state of world affairs after the collapse of the USSR at the end of the Cold War and in the context of using international organizations to assist in governing international relations. The term **One World Government** is also used as a synonym for the New World Order.

charter; 4) only *approved* churches and other places of worship will be permitted to operate and will become appendages of the One World Religion, which will be the only legitimate doctrine of religious beliefs and ethical values; 5) home schooling will be outlawed and all school curriculum will need to be approved by the United Nations Educational, Scientific, and Cultural Organization (UNESCO); and 6) American military bases and other federal facilities will be used as concentration camps by the U.N. to confine those patriots, including the militias, who defy the NWO. Other groups beside the U.N. that are often mentioned as being part of the NWO conspiracy theory are Jews, communists, the Council on Foreign Relations, the Bilderbergers, and the Trilateral Commission. Law enforcement officials will probably notice different versions of this theory, depending upon the source.

The NWO conspiracy theory is particularly relevant to the millennium because the year 2000 is considered to be a triggering device for the NWO due to the element of computer breakdown. Many computers around the world are based on a numerical system in which the year is only registered by the last two digits. A number of militia members accept the theory that on January 1, 2000, many computers will misinterpret this date as January 1, 1900, and malfunction and/or shut down completely. They further believe that these major computer malfunctions will cause widespread chaos at all levels of society — economic, social, and political. This chaos will theoretically create a situation in which American civilization will collapse, which will then produce an environment that the U.N. will exploit to forcibly take over the United States. Therefore, these militia members (as well as other groups) believe that the year 2000 will be the catalyst for the NWO.

According to James Wickstrom, former leader of the defunct Posse Comitatus and "Minister" of the True Church of Israel, anyone who holds any powerful political influence knows that the Y2K crisis may be the final fuse that will lead to the NWO that "David Rockefeller and the rest of his satanic jew seedline desire to usher in upon the earth."[15] He claims that Jews have conspired to create the Y2K problem and that the prospect of impending computer failure is very real. Similarly, *The New American,* an organ of the ultra-conservative John Birch Society, speculates that the Y2K bug could be America's Reichstag fire, a reference to the 1933 arson attack on Germany's Parliament building that was used by Hitler as an excuse to enact police state laws. Similar to this train of thought, Norm Olson, leader of the Northern Michigan Regional Militia, believes constitutional rights probably will be suspended before the real crisis hits. He states: "It will be the worst time for humanity since the Noahic flood."[16]

However, there are some extremists who do not attach any major significance to the Y2K problem. In his article, "The Millennium Bug and 'Mainstreaming' the News," William Pierce of the National Alliance tells his followers not to worry, or at least, not to worry very much about the Y2K issue. Pierce predicts that the main event that will occur on New Year's Day 2000 is that crazed millennialists will go "berserk when the Second Coming fails to occur." Also, "a few right-wing nuts may launch a premature attack on the government, figuring that without its computers the government won't be able to fight back." Pierce claims that the lights will remain on, and that airplanes will not fall from the sky. He says that he is able to make such a prediction with some degree of confidence because, "contrary to what some cranks would have you believe, the computer professionals and the government have been working on the Y2K problem for some time."[17]

---

15. James P. Wickstrom, "Intelligence Update," October 1998, accessed at *www.posse-comitatus.org.*

16. See Fall 1998 edition of the Southern Poverty Law Center's *Intelligence Report,* "Millennium Y2KAOS."

17. William Pierce, "The Millennium Bug and 'Mainstreaming' the News," accessed at *www.natvan.com.*

Gun Control Laws

The passage of the Brady Bill and assault weapons ban in 1994 were interpreted by those in the militia movement and among the right-wing as the first steps toward disarming citizens in preparation for the U.N.-led NWO takeover. Some are convinced that the registration of gun owners is in preparation for a confiscation of firearms and eventually the arrest of the gun owners themselves. An article by Larry Pratt, Executive Director for Gun Owners of America, interprets a 1995 U.N. study of small arms, done reportedly in cooperation with U.S. police, customs, and military services, as part of the U.N.'s plan to take over the U.S. Pratt goes on to say that the "U.N. is increasingly assuming the jurisdictional authority of a federal world government with the U.S. as just one of scores of member states. And gun control — meaning civilian disarmament — is high up on the agenda of the U.N."[18] Speculation like this only serves to fuel the already existing paranoia of militia and patriot groups.

The right-wing believes that many of the restrictions being placed on the ownership of firearms today mirror events in *The Turner Diaries*. In his book, Pierce writes about the United States government banning the private possession of firearms and staging gun raids in an effort to arrest gun owners. The book discusses the government/police use of black men, assigned as "special deputies" to carry out the gun raids. Many members of the right-wing movement view the book as prophetic, believing that it is only a matter of time before these events occur in real life.

In the aftermath of the school shootings in Littleton, Colorado, President Clinton, Congress, and Attorney General Janet Reno acted swiftly to propose new laws aimed at restricting the sales of guns to juveniles and to close loopholes in existing laws. In May 1999, the Senate passed a bill to ban the importation of high capacity ammunition magazines and require background checks for guns sold at

---

18. Larry Pratt, "The United Nations: Pressing for U.S. Gun Control," accessed at *www.gunowners.org*.

gun shows. In light of the enormous importance and prominent role that extremist groups place on the Second Amendment, it is probable that recent government actions aimed at controlling guns are perceived to be compelling signs of the U.N.-led NWO takeover.

III. CHRISTIAN IDENTITY

Christian Identity is an ideology which asserts that the white Aryan race is God's chosen race and that whites comprise the ten lost tribes of Israel.[19] There is no single document that expresses this belief system. Adherents refer to the Bible to justify their racist ideals. Interpreting the Book of Genesis, Christian Identity followers assert that Adam was preceded by other, lesser races, identified as "the beasts of the field" (Gen. 1:25). Eve was seduced by the snake (Satan) and gave birth to two seed lines: Cain, the direct descendant of Satan and Eve, and Abel, who was of good Aryan stock through Adam. Cain then became the progenitor of the Jews in his subsequent matings with the non-Adamic races. Christian Identity adherents believe the Jews are predisposed to carry on a conspiracy against the Adamic seed line and today have achieved almost complete control of the earth.[20] This is referred to as the two-seedline doctrine, which provides Christian Identity followers with a biblical justification for hatred.

The roots of the Christian Identity movement can be traced back to British-Israelism, the conviction that the British are the lineal descendants of the "ten lost tribes" of Israel. It is a belief that exist-

---

19. There were twelve tribes of Israel, but they were divided into two different kingdoms after the death of King Solomon. The northern kingdom was called "Israel" and consisted of ten tribes and the southern kingdom was called "Judah" and was comprised of two tribes. There is a record of the two tribes making up the southern kingdom, but the ten northern tribes were "lost" after they were conquered around 722 B.C. by the Assyrians.
20. Jeffrey Kaplan, *Radical Religion in America* (Syracuse, N.Y.: Syracuse University Press, 1997), pp. 47–48.

ed for some time before it became a movement in the second half of the nineteenth century. The writings of John Wilson helped to extend the idea of British-Israelism to Anglo-Israelism, which included other Teutonic peoples — mostly northern European peoples from Germany, Italy, France, and Switzerland. British–Israelism was brought to America in the early part of the 1920s, where it remained decentralized until the 1930s. At that time, the movement underwent the final transformation to become what we know as Christian Identity, at which time its ties to the original English movement were cut and it became distinctly American.

Wesley Swift is considered the single most significant figure in the early years of the Christian Identity movement in the United States. He popularized it in the right-wing by "combining British-Israelism, a demonic anti-Semitism, and political extremism."[21] He founded his own church in California in the mid 1940s where he could preach this ideology. In addition, he had a daily radio broadcast in California during the 1950s and '60s, through which he was able to proclaim his ideology to a large audience. With Swift's efforts, the message of his church spread, leading to the creation of similar churches throughout the country. In 1957, the name of his church was changed to The Church of Jesus Christ Christian, which is used today by Aryan Nations (AN) churches.

One of Swift's associates, Wiliam Potter Gale, was far more militant than Swift and brought a new element to Christian Identity churches. He became a leading figure in the anti-tax and paramilitary movements of the 1970s and '80s. There are numerous Christian Identity churches that preach similar messages and some espouse more violent rhetoric than others, but all hold fast to the belief that Aryans are God's chosen race.

Christian Identity also believes in the inevitability of the end of the world and the Second Coming of Christ. It is believed that these

---

21. Michael Barkun, *Religion and the Racist Right* (Chapel Hill, N.C.: The University of North Carolina Press, 1997), p. 60.

events are part of a cleansing process that is needed before Christ's kingdom can be established on earth. During this time, Jews and their allies will attempt to destroy the white race using any means available. The result will be a violent and bloody struggle — a war, in effect — between God's forces, the white race, and the forces of evil, the Jews and nonwhites. Significantly, many adherents believe that this will be tied into the coming of the new millennium.

The view of what Armageddon will be varies among Christian Identity believers. Some contend there will be a race war in which millions will die; others believe that the United Nations, backed by Jewish representatives of the anti-Christ, will take over the country and promote a New World Order. One Christian Identity interpretation is that white Christians have been chosen to watch for signs of the impending war in order to warn others. They are to then physically struggle with the forces of evil against sin and other violations of God's law (i.e., race-mixing and internationalism); many will perish, and some of God's chosen will be forced to wear the Mark of the Beast to participate in business and commerce. After the final battle is ended and God's kingdom is established on earth, only then will the Aryan people be recognized as the one and true Israel.

Christian Identity adherents believe that God will use his chosen race as his weapons to battle the forces of evil. Christian Identity followers believe they are among those chosen by God to wage this battle during Armageddon and they will be the last line of defense for the white race and Christian America. To prepare for these events, they engage in survivalist and paramilitary training, storing foodstuffs and supplies, and caching weapons and ammunition. They often reside on compounds located in remote areas.

As the millennium approaches, various right-wing groups pose a threat to American society. The radical right encompasses a vast number and variety of groups, such as survivalists, militias, the Ku Klux Klan, neo-Nazis, Christian Identity churches, the AN, and skinheads. These groups are not mutually exclusive and within the subculture individuals easily migrate from one group to another. This intermixing of organizations makes it difficult to discern a singular religious ideology or belief system that encompasses the right-wing.

Nevertheless, Christian Identity is the most unifying theology for a number of these diverse groups and one widely adhered to by white supremacists. It is a belief system that provides its members with a religious basis for racism and an ideology that condones violence against non-Aryans. This doctrine allows believers to fuse religion with hate, conspiracy theories, and apocalyptic fear of the future. Christian Identity-inspired millennialism has a distinctly racist tinge in the belief that Armageddon will be a race war of Aryans against Jews and nonwhites. The potential difficulty society may face due to the Y2K computer glitch is considered by a number of Christian Identity adherents to be the perfect event upon which to instigate a race war.

There are a number of issues concerning the Christian Identity belief system that create problems when determining the threat level of groups. First, Christian Identity does not have a national organizational structure. Rather, it is a grouping of churches throughout the country which follows its basic ideology. Some of these churches can be as small as a dozen people, and some as large as the AN church, which claims membership in the thousands. In addition, some groups take the belief to a higher extreme and believe violence is the means to achieve their goal. This lack of structure creates a greater potential for violent actions by lone offenders and/or leaderless cells. It is important to note that only a small percentage of Christian Identity adherents believe that the new millennium will bring about a race war. However, those that do have a high propensity for violence.

Secondly, there are many factions of the right-wing, from Christian Identity to militias, all of which are intermingled in ideology and members. In some cases it is easy for a person to be a member of more than one group or to move from one to another. Often, if a member of one group believes the group is lax in its convictions, he or she will gravitate to a group that is more radical.

The third concern is the increased level of cooperation between the different groups. This trend can be seen throughout the right-wing. Christian Identity followers are pairing up with militias to receive paramilitary training and have also joined with members of the Ku Klux Klan and other right-wing groups. This cohesiveness creates an environment in which ideology can easily spread and branch out. However, it makes the job of law enforcement much more difficult as there are no distinctive borders between groups or ideology.

Lastly, the formation of splinter groups or state chapters from larger organizations presents an increased level of threat due to the likelihood that the leader has diminished control over the members and actions of the smaller groups. The AN is a large group that adheres to the Christian Identity belief system. The group espouses hatred toward Jews, the federal government, blacks, and other minorities. The ultimate goal of the AN is to forcibly take five northwestern states — Oregon, Idaho, W yoming, Washington, and Montana — from the United States government in order to establish an Aryan homeland. It consists of a headquarters in Hayden Lake, Idaho, and a number of state chapters, which often act as their own entities. While the leader may not support or encourage acts of violence, it is easy for small cells of members or splinter groups to take part in violent acts without the knowledge of the leader. The individuals are associated with the group as a whole and carry the name of the group, but many perpetrate acts on their own.

These factors make a threat assessment concerning millennial violence difficult to determine. There is a moderate possibility of small factions of right-wing groups, whether they be members of the same group, or members of different groups, acting in an overtly violent manner in order to initiate the Apocalypse.

Several problems associated with the assessment for violence can be seen when looking at the structure and actions of the AN. The AN has been headquartered at Hayden Lake since the late 1970s and remains a focal point for the group's activities. Its annual World Congress attracts a number of different factions from the right-wing, including members and leaders of various right-wing groups. The World Congress is often viewed as a sort of round table to discuss right-wing issues. These meetings have led to an increased level of contact between AN members and members and leaders of other groups. This degree of networking within the right-wing may further the AN's base of support and help advance its cause.

One of the greatest threats posed by the right-wing in terms of millennial violence is the formation of a conglomeration of individuals that will work together to commit criminal acts. This has happened with some frequency in the past. Bob Mathews formed a subgroup of the AN, called The Order, which committed a number of violent crimes, including murder. Their mission was to bring about a race war and there are several groups that currently exist which hold these same beliefs. Dennis McGiffen, who also had ties to the AN, formed a cell called The New Order, based on Mathews' group. The members were arrested before they could follow through on their plans to try to start a race war. Chevie Kehoe, who was convicted of three homicides, conspiracy, and interstate transportation of stolen property, also spent some time at the AN compound. Most recently, Buford O. Furrow, Jr., the man accused of the August 10, 1999, shooting at the Jewish Community Center in Los Angeles, California, also spent some time at the AN compound working as a security guard.

A relatively new tenet gaining popularity among Christian Identity believers justifies the use of violence if it is perpetrated in order to punish violators of God's law, as found in the Bible and interpreted by Christian Identity ministers and adherents. This includes killing interracial couples, abortionists, prostitutes and homosexuals, burning pornography stores, and robbing banks and perpetrating frauds to undermine the "usury system." Christian Identity adherents engaging in such behavior are referred to as Phineas Priests or members of the Phineas Priesthood. This is a very appealing concept to Christian Identity's extremist members who believe they are being persecuted by the Jewish-controlled U.S. government and society and/or are eagerly preparing for Armageddon. Among adherents today, the Phineas Priesthood is viewed as a call to action or a badge of honor.

IV. WHITE SUPREMACY

There are a number of white supremacy groups that do not necessarily adhere to Christian Identity or other religious doctrines. White supremacy groups such as the National Alliance, the American Nazi Party, and the National Socialist White People's Party, are largely politically, rather than religiously, motivated.

The National Alliance is probably best known for its leader, William Pierce, who is one of the most recognized names in the radical right. Pierce wrote *The Turner Diaries* and *Hunter* and hosts a weekly radio program, *American Dissident Voices*. Via these outlets, Pierce is able to provide his followers with an ideological and practical framework for committing violent acts. The rhetoric of these groups largely shadows that of Adolf Hitler's in content and political ideology. In 1997, Pierce stated that:

> Ultimately we must separate ourselves from the Blacks and other nonwhites and keep ourselves separate, no matter what it takes to accomplish this. We must do this not because we hate Blacks, but because we cannot survive if we remain mixed with them. And we cannot survive if we permit the Jews and the traitors among us to remain among us and to repeat their treachery. Eventually we must hunt them down and get rid of them.[22]

The end goal of National Socialist and Christian Identity devotees is the same: an all white nation. However, Christian Identity followers appear to be more of a threat concerning the millennium be-

---

22. Anti-Defamation League, *Explosion of Hate,* p. 15.

cause of their religious beliefs.

There are also white supremacist groups which adhere to the general supremacist ideology, but are not political or religious in nature. For example, The Ku Klux Klan (KKK) proposes racial segregation that is not generally based on religious ideals. The KKK is one of the most recognized white supremacist groups in the United States. Its history is expansive and its actions of cross burnings and rhetoric of hate are well known. There is currently not a singular KKK group with a hierarchical structure, but many different KKK groups with a common ideology.

The KKK, as a whole, does not pose a significant threat with regard to the millennium. That is not to say that a member of the KKK will not act on his own or in concert with members of another group. Law enforcement has been very successful in infiltrating a number of these groups, thereby keeping abreast of their plans for action. The KKK also draws the attention of many watchdog groups, and the Southern Poverty Law Center produces a quarterly publication entitled *Klanwatch*. It would be difficult for any of the known KKK groups to participate in millennial violence without law enforcement knowing.

Again, there is a great deal of movement that is possible throughout the right-wing, regardless of prior beliefs. If a member of a Christian Identity faction does not feel that his current group is taking enough violent action, it is possible for that member to move on to other ideologies or organizations such as Odinism, the World Church of the Creator (WCOTC) or the National Socialist movement. Because of this movement, it is also likely that communication exists between various factions of the right-wing, from religious groups to skinheads. Their end goals are similar.

The WCOTC presents a recent example of violence perpetrated by a white supremacist in order to bring about a race war. The major creed upon which Ben Klassen founded the religion is that one's race is his religion. Aside from this central belief, its ideology is similar to many Christian Identity groups in the conviction that there is a Jewish conspiracy in control of the federal government, international banking, and the media. They also dictate that RAHOWA, a racial holy war, is destined to ensue to rid the world of Jews and "mud races." In the early 1990s, there was a dramatic increase in membership due to the growing belief in the Apocalypse and that RAHOWA was imminent.

In 1996, Matt Hale, who has come upon recent fame by being denied a license to practice law in Illinois, was appointed the new leader of the Church of the Creator. Hale made a number of changes to the group, including changing the name of the organization to the World Church of the Creator, giving it the feel of a widespread movement.

As publicly reported, there is information to indicate that the WCOTC has violent plans for the millennium. Officials who searched Benjamin Smith's apartment, the man who went on a racially motivated killing spree over the Fourth of July weekend, found a loose-leaf binder of handwritings. These writings described a holy war among the races and included a reference to the new millennium. Passages included plans of how white supremacists would shoot at nonwhites from motor vehicles after the dawning of the new millennium.[23] While the group's rhetoric does include the belief in a race war and the creation of an all white bastion within the United States, other than Smith's writings, there is no indication that it is linked to the millennium.

In addition, there have been recent incidents that have demonstrated the willingness of members to take part in violent action. WCOTC members in Southern Florida are thought to be tied to several racially motivated beatings. Within the last year, four Florida members were convicted for the pistol-whipping and robbery of a Jewish video store owner. They were supposedly trying to raise money for "the revolution."[24]

---

23. "U.S. Mulls Church Probe; Ties to Killings Investigated," *Chicago Tribune,* July 9, 1999.

24. "Behind the Hate," *Washington Post,* July 6, 1999.

Finally, Odinism is another white supremacist ideology that lends itself to violence and has the potential to inspire its followers to violence in connection to the millennium. What makes Odinists dangerous is the fact that many believe in the necessity of becoming martyrs for their cause. For example, Bob Mathews, the leader of The Order, died in a fiery confrontation with law enforcement. Also, William King relished the fact that he would receive the death penalty for his act of dragging James Byrd, Jr., to his death. Odinism has little to do with Christian Identity but there is one key similarity: Odinism provides dualism — as does Christian Identity — with regard to the universe being made up of worlds of light (white people) and worlds of dark (nonwhite people). The most fundamental difference between the two ideologies is that Odinists do not believe in Jesus Christ. However, there are enough similarities between the myths and legends of Odinism and the beliefs of Christian Identity to make a smooth transition from Christian Identity to Odinism for those racist individuals whose penchant for violence is not being satisfied.

V. MILITIAS

The majority of growth within the militia movement occurred during the 1990s. There is not a simple definition of how a group qualifies as a militia. However, the following general criteria can be used as a guideline: 1) a militia is a domestic organization with two or more members; 2) the organization must possess and use firearms; and 3) the organization must conduct or encourage paramilitary training. Other terms used to describe militias are Patriots and Minutemen.

Most militias engage in a variety of anti-government rhetoric. This discourse can range from the protesting of government policies to the advocating of violence and/or the overthrow of the federal government. However, the majority of militia groups are non-violent and only a small segment of the militias actually commit acts of violence to advance their political goals and beliefs. A number of militia leaders, such as Lynn Van Huizen of the Michigan Militia Corps – Wolverines, have gone to some effort to actively rid their ranks of radical members who are inclined to carry out acts of violence and/or terrorism.[25] Officials at the FBI Academy classify militia groups within four categories, ranging from moderate groups who do not engage in criminal activity to radical cells which commit violent acts of terrorism.[26] It should be clearly stated that the FBI only focuses on *radical elements* of the militia movement capable and willing to commit violence against government, law enforcement, civilian, military, and international targets. In addition, any such investigation of these radical militia units must be conducted within strict legal parameters.

Militia anxiety and paranoia specifically relating to the year 2000 are based mainly on a political ideology, as opposed to religious beliefs. Many militia members believe that the year 2000 will lead to political and personal repression enforced by the United Nations and countenanced by a compliant U.S. government. This belief is commonly known as the New World Order (NWO) conspiracy theory (see Chapter I, Introduction). Other issues which have served as motivating factors for the militia movement include gun control, the incidents at Ruby Ridge (1992) and Waco (1993), the Montana Freemen Standoff (1996), and the restriction of land use by federal agencies.

One component of the NWO conspiracy theory — that of the use of American military bases by the U.N. — is worth exploring in further detail. Law enforcement officers, as well as military personnel, should be aware that the nation's armed forces have been the subject of a great deal of rumor and paranoia circulating among many militia groups. One can find numerous references in militia literature to military bases to be used as concentration camps in

---

25. Van Huizen lost re-election as commander of the MMCW in late 1997 to the more radical Joe Pilchak.
26. See "Militias — Initiating Contact," *FBI Law Enforcement Bulletin,* July 1997, pp. 22–26.

the NWO and visiting foreign military personnel conspiring to attack Americans. One example of this can be found on the website for the militia group United States Theatre Command (USTC).[27] The USTC website prominently features the NWO theory as it portrays both Camp Grayling in Michigan and Fort Dix in New Jersey as detention centers to be used to house prisoners in an upcoming war. Specifically in reference to a photograph of Camp Grayling, the USTC website states: "Note that the barbed wire is configured to keep people *in,* not *out,* and also note in the middle of the guard towers, a platform for the mounting of a machine gun." Specifically in reference to a photograph of Fort Dix, the USTC website states: "Actual photos of an 'Enemy Prisoner of War' camp in the United States of America! (Fort Dix, New Jersey, to be exact!) Is there going to be a war here? Many more are suspected to be scattered throughout the United States."

Law enforcement personnel should be aware of the fact that the majority of militias are *reactive,* as opposed to *proactive. Reactive* militia groups are generally not a threat to law enforcement or the public. These militias may indeed believe that some type of NWO scenario may be imminent in the year 2000, but they are more inclined to sit back and wait for it to happen. They will stockpile their guns and ammunition and food, and wait for the government to curtain their liberties and take away their guns. When the expected NWO tragedy does not take place, these *reactive* militias will simply continue their current activities, most of which are relatively harmless. They will not overreact to minor disruptions of electricity, water, and other public services.

However, there is a small percentage of the militia movement which may be more *proactive* and commit acts of domestic terrorism. As stated earlier, the main focus of the militias connected to the Y2K/millennium revolves around the NWO conspiracy theory. While the NWO is a paranoid theory, there may be some real tech-

---

27. Accessed at *www.eagleflt.com.*

nological problems arising from the year 2000. Among these are malfunctioning computers, which control so many facets of our everyday lives. Any such computer malfunctions may adversely affect power stations and other critical infrastructure. If such breakdowns do occur, these may be interpreted as a sign by some of the militias that electricity is being shut off on purpose in order to create an environment of confusion. In the paranoid rationalizations of these militia groups, this atmosphere of confusion can only be a prelude to the dreaded NWO/One World Government. These groups may then follow through on their premeditated plans of action.

VI. BLACK HEBREW ISRAELITES

As the millennium approaches, radical fringe members of the Black Hebrew Israelite (BHI) movement may pose a challenge for law enforcement. As with the adherents of most apocalyptic philosophies, certain segments of the BHI movement have the potential to engage in violence at the turn of the century. This movement has been associated with extreme acts of violence in the recent past, and current intelligence from a variety of sources indicates that extreme factions of BHI groups are preparing for a race war to close the millennium.

Violent BHI followers can generally be described as proponents of an extreme form of black supremacy. Drawing upon the teachings of earlier BHI adherents, such groups hold that blacks represent God's true "chosen people," while condemning whites as incarnate manifestations of evil. As God's "authentic" Jews, BHI adherents believe that mainstream Jews are actually imposters. Such beliefs bear a striking resemblance to the Christian Identity theology practiced by many white supremacists. In fact, Tom Metzger, renowned white supremacist, once remarked, "They're the black counterpart of us."[28] Like their Christian Identity counterparts, militant BHI

28. See Fall 1997 edition of the Southern Poverty Law Center's *Intelligence Report,* "Rough Waters: Stream of Knowledge Probed by Officials."

followers tend to see themselves as divinely endowed by God with superior status. As a result, some followers of this belief system hold that violence, including murder, is justifiable in the eyes of God, provided that it helps to rid the world of evil. Violent BHI groups are of particular concern as the millennium approaches because they believe in the inevitability of a race war between blacks and whites.

The extreme elements of the BHI movement are prone to engage in violent activity. As seen in previous convictions of BHI followers, adherents of this philosophy have a proven history of violence, and several indications point toward a continuation of this trend. Some BHI followers have been observed in public donning primarily black clothing, with emblems and/or patches bearing the "Star of David" symbol. Some BHI members practice paramilitary operations and wear web belts and shoulder holsters. Some adherents have extensive criminal records for a variety of violations, including weapons charges, assault, drug trafficking, and fraud.

In law enforcement circles, BHI groups are typically associated with violence and criminal activity, largely as a result of the movement's popularization by Yahwey Ben Yahweh, formerly known as Hulon Mitchell, Jr., and the Miami-based Nation of Yahwey (NOY). In reality, the origins of the BHI movement are non-violent. While the BHI belief system may have roots in the United States as far back as the Civil War era, the movement became more recognized as a result of the teachings of an individual known as Ben Ami Ben Israel, a.k.a. Ben Carter, from the south side of Chicago. Ben Israel claims to have had a vision at the age of twenty-seven, hearing "a voice tell me that the time had come for Africans in America, the descendants of the Biblical Israelites, to return to the land of our forefathers."[29] Ben Israel persuaded a group of African-Americans to accompany him to Israel in 1967, teaching that African-Ameri-

29. Linda Jones, "Claiming a Promised Land: African-American settlers in Israel are guided by idea of independent Black Hebrew Society," *Dallas Morning News,* July 27, 1997.

cans descended from the biblical tribe of Judah and, therefore, that Israel is the land of their birthright. Ben Israel and his followers initially settled in Liberia for the purposes of cleansing themselves of bad habits. In 1969, a small group of BHI followeres left Liberia for Israel, with Ben Israel and the remaining original migrants arriving in Israel the following year. Public source estimates of the BHI community in Israel number between 1,500 and 3,000.[30] Despite promoting non-violence, members of Ben Israel's movement have shown a willingness to engage in criminal activity. For example, in 1986, Ben Israel and his top aide, Prince Asiel Ben Israel, were convicted of trafficking stolen passports and securities and forging checks and savings bonds.[31]

BHI in Israel are generally peaceful, if somewhat controversial. The FBI has no information to indicate that Ben Israel's BHI community in Israel is planning any activity — terrorist, criminal, or otherwise — inspired by the coming millennium. Ben Israel's claims to legitimate Judaism have at times caused consternation to the Israeli government. BHI adherents in Israel have apparently espoused anti-Semitic remarks, labeling Israeli Jews as "imposters."[32] Neither the Israeli government nor the Orthodox rabbinate recognize the legitimacy of BHI claims to Judaism. According to Jewish law, an individual can be recognized as Jewish if he/she was born to a Jewish mother or if the individual agrees to convert to Judaism.[33] At present, BHI in Israel have legal status as temporary residents, which gives them the right to work and live in Israel, but not to vote. They are not considered to be Israeli citizens. While BHI claims to Judaism are disregarded by Israeli officials and religious leaders,

30. Ibid.
31. See Fall 1997 Southern Poverty Law Center's *Intelligence Report,* "Rough Waters: Stream of Knowledge Probed by Officials."
32. Jones, *Dallas Morning News,* July 27, 1997.
33. Ibid.

the BHI community is tolerated and appears to be peaceful.[34]

While the BHI community in Israel is peaceful, BHI adherents in the United States became associated with violence thanks to the rise of the NOY, which reached the height of its popularity in the 1980s. The NOY was founded in 1979 and led by Yahweh Ben Yahweh. Ben Yahweh's followers viewed him as the Messiah, and therefore demonstrated unrequited and unquestioned obedience. Members of the organization engaged in numerous acts of violence in the 1980s, including several homicides, following direct orders from Ben Yahweh. Seventeen NOY members were indicted by a federal grand jury in Miami in 1990–91 on charges of RICO, RICO conspiracy, and various racketeering acts. Various members were convicted on RICO conspiracy charges and remain imprisoned.

While the overwhelming majority of BHI followers are unlikely to engage in violence, there are elements of this movement with both the motivation and the capability to engage in millennial violence. Some radical BHI adherents are clearly motivated by the conviction that the approach of the year 2000 brings society ever closer to a violent confrontation between blacks and whites. While the rhetoric professed by various BHI groups is fiery and threatening, there are no indications of explicitly identified targets for violence, beyond a general condemnation and demonization of whites and "imposter" Jews. Militant BHI groups tend to distrust the United States government; however, there are no specific indications of imminent violence toward the government.

VII. APOCALYPTIC CULTS

For apocalyptic cults, especially biblically based ones, the millennium is viewed as the time that will signal a major transformation for the world. Many apocalyptic cults share the belief that the battle

---

34. Ibid. In fact, in the community of Dimona where the BHI community resides, the Dimona Police Chief spoke in complimentary terms as to the group's discipline, leadership, and integrity.

against Satan, as prophesied in the Book of Revelation, will begin in the years surrounding the millennium and that the federal government is an arm of Satan. Therefore, the millennium will bring about a battle between cult members — religious martyrs — and the government.

In the broadest meaning, cults are composed of individuals who demonstrate "great devotion to a person, idea, object, or movement."[35] However, using that definition, many domestic terrorist groups could be characterized as cults, including Christian Identity churches, Black Hebrew Israelites, and some militias. For law enforcement purposes, a narrower interpretation of groups that qualify as cults is needed. A more useful definition of cults incorporates the term "cultic relationships" to describe the interactions within a cult.[36] Specifically, a cultic relationship refers to "one in which a person intentionally induces others to become totally or nearly totally dependent on him or her for almost all major life decisions, and inculcates in these followers a belief that he or she has some special talent, gift, or knowledge."[37] This definition of cults provides important distinctions that are vital for analyzing a cult's predilection toward violence.

The origin of the cult, the role of its leader, and its uniqueness provide a framework for understanding what distinguishes cults from other domestic terrorist groups that otherwise share many similar characteristics. These distinctions are: 1) cult leaders are self-appointed, persuasive persons who claim to have a special mission in life or have special knowledge; 2) a cult's ideas and dogma claim to be innovative and exclusive; and 3) cult leaders focus their mem-

---

35. Frederick C. Mish, ed., *Merriam Webster's Collegiate Dictionary 10th Edition* (Springfield, MA: Merriam-Webster, Incorporated, 1997), p. 282.

36. Margaret Thaler Singer and Janja Lalich, *Cults in Our Midst: The Hidden Menace in Our Everday* (San Francisco, CA: Jossey-Bass Publishers, 1995), p. 7.

37. Ibid., p. 7

bers' love, devotion, and allegiance on themselves.[38] These characteristics culminate in a group structure that is frequently highly authoritarian in structure. Such a structure is a sharp contrast to the rapidly emerging trend among domestic terrorist groups toward a leaderless, non–authoritarian structure.

While predicting violence is extremely difficult and imprecise, there are certain characteristics that make some cults more prone to violence. Law enforcement officials should be aware of the following factors:

- **Sequestered Groups:** Members of sequestered groups lose access to the outside world and information preventing critical evaluation of the ideas being espoused by the leader.
- **Leader's History:** The fantasies, dreams, plans, and ideas of the leader are most likely to become the beliefs of the followers because of the totalitarian and authoritarian nature of cults.
- **Psychopaths:** Control of a group by charismatic psychopaths or those with narcissistic character disorders.
- **Changes in the Leader:** Changes in a leader's personality caused by traumatic events such as death of a spouse or sickness.
- **Language of the Ideology:** Groups that are violent use language in their ideology that contains the seeds of violence.
- **Implied Directive for Violence:** Most frequently, a leader's speeches, rhetoric, and language does not explicitly call for violence, rather it is most often only implied.
- **Length of Time:** The longer the leader's behavior has gone unchecked against outside authority, the less vulnerable the leader feels.
- **Who Is in the Inner Circle:** Cults with violent tendencies often recruit people who are either familiar with weapons or who have military backgrounds to serve as enforcers.

---

38. Ibid., pp. 8–9.

Apocalyptic cults see their mission in two general ways: They either want to accelerate the end of time or take action to ensure that they survive the millennium. For example, Aum Shinrikyo wanted to take action to hasten the end of the world, while compounds in general are built to survive the endtime safely. An analysis of millennial cults by the FBI's Behavioral Science Unit describes how rhetoric changes depending on whether the leader's ideology envisions the group as playing an active role in the coming Apocalypse or a passive survivalist role:

> A cult that predicts that "God will punish" or "evil will be punished" indicates a more passive and less threatening posture than the cult that predicts that "God's chosen people will punish. . . ." As another example, the members of a passive group might predict that God or another being will one day liberate their souls from their bodies or come to carry them away. The followers of a more action-oriented group would, in contrast, predict that they themselves will one day shed their mortal bodies or transport themselves to another place.[39]

A cult that displays these characteristics may then produce three social-psychological components, referred to as the "Lethal Triad," that predispose a cult toward violence aimed at its members and/or outsiders.[40] Cults in which members are heavily dependent on the leader for all decision making almost always physically and psychologically isolate their members from outsiders, the first component of the triad.[41] The other two components interact in the following way:

---

39. Carl J. Jensen, III, Rod Gregg and Adam Szubin, "When a Cult Comes to Town," accessed from Law Enforcement Online.
40. Kevin M. Gilmartin, "The Lethal Triad: Understanding the Nature of Isolated Extremist Groups," *www.leo.gov/tlib/leb/1996/sept961/txt.*
41. Carl J. Jenson, III and Yvonne Hsieh, "Law Enforcement and the Millennialist Vision: A Behavioral Approach," accessed from Law Enforcement Online.

... **isolation** causes a reduction of critical thinking on the part of group members who become entrenched in the belief proposed by the group leadership. As a result, group members relinquish all responsibility for group decision making to their leader and blame the cause of all group grievances on some outside entity or force, a process known as projection. Finally, isolation and **projection** combine to produce pathological **anger**, the final component of the triad.[42]

Of the nearly one thousand cults operating in the United States, very few present credible threats for millennial violence. Law enforcement officials should concentrate on those cults that advocate force or violence to achieve their goals concerning the endtime, as well as those cults which possess a substantial number of the distinguished traits listed above.[43] In particular, cults of greatest concern to law enforcement are those that: 1) believe they play a special, elite role in the endtime; 2) believe violent offensive action is needed to fulfill their endtime prophecy; 3) take steps to attain their

---

42. Ibid.
43. B. A. Robinson in "Factors Commonly Found in Doomsday Cults," identifies traits that provide a framework for analyzing cults. They include the following: 1) The leader preaches end of the world/Armageddon in 2000 or within a reasonable time frame before and after 2000; 2) the cult expects to play a major, elite role at the endtime; 3) the cult has large numbers of firearms, explosives, or weapons of mass destruction; 4) the cult has prepared defensive structures; 5) the cult speaks of offensive action; 6) the cult is led by a single male charismatic leader; 7) the leader dominates the membership through physical, sexual, and emotional control; 8) the cult is not an established denomination; 9) cult members live together in a community isolated from society; 10) extreme paranoia exists within the cult concerning the monitoring by outsiders and government persecution; 11) and outsiders are distrusted and disliked. These factors are designed to leave out cults that have unique endtime beliefs, but whose ideology does not include the advocacy of force or violence.

beliefs. Those factors may culminate in plans to initiate conflict with outsiders or law enforcement.

The violent tendencies of dangerous cults can be classified into two general categories — defensive violence or offensive violence. Defensive violence is utilized by cults to defend a compound or enclave that was created specifically to eliminate most contact with the dominant culture.[44] The 1993 clash in Waco, Texas, at the Branch Davidian complex is an illustration of such defensive violence. History has shown that groups that seek to withdraw from the dominant culture seldom act on their beliefs that the endtime has come unless provoked.[45]

Cults with an apocalyptic agenda, particularly those that appear ready to *initiate* rather than *anticipate* violent confrontations to bring about Armageddon or fulfill "prophecy" present unique challenges to law enforcement officials. One example of this type of group is the Concerned Christians (CC). Monte Kim Miller, the CC leader, claims to be one of the two witnesses or prophets described in the Book of Revelation who will die on the streets of Jerusalem prior to the second coming of Christ. To attain that result, members of the CC traveled to Israel in 1998 in the belief that Miller would be killed in a violent confrontation in the streets of Jerusalem in December 1999. CC members believe that Miller's death will set off an apocalyptic end to the millennium, at which time all of Miller's followers will be sent to Heaven. Miller has convinced his followers that America is "Babylon the Great" referred to in the Book of Revelation. In early October 1998, CC members suddenly vanished from the United States, an apparent response to one of Miller's "prophecies" that Denver would be destroyed on October 10, 1998. In January 1999, fourteen members of the group who had moved to Jerusalem were deported by the Israeli government on the grounds that

44. Jeffrey Kaplan, *Radical Religion in America,* p. 57.
45. Ibid., p. 165.

they were preparing to hasten the fulfillment of Miller's prophecies by instigating violence.[46]

Ascertaining the intentions of such cults is a daunting endeavor, particularly since the agenda or plan of a cult is often at the whim of its leader. Law enforcement personnel should become well acquainted with the previously mentioned indicators of potential cult violence in order to separate the violent from the non-violent.

VIII. THE SIGNIFICANCE OF JERUSALEM

The city of Jerusalem, cherished by Jews, Christians, and Muslims alike, faces many serious challenges as the year 2000 approaches. As already evidenced by the deportation of various members of the religious cult known as the Concerned Christians, zealotry from all three major monotheistic religions is particularly acute in Israel, where holy shrines, temples, churches, and mosques are located. While events surrounding the millennium in Jerusalem are much more problematic for the Israeli government than for the United States, the potential for violent acts in Jerusalem will cause reverberations around the world, including the United States. The extreme terrorist fringes of Christianity, Judaism, and Islam are all present in the United States. Thus, millennial violence in Jerusalem could conceivably lead to violence in the United States as well.

Within Jerusalem, the Temple Mount, or Haram al-Sharif, holds a special significance for both Muslims and Jews.[47] The Temple Mount houses the third holiest of all Islamic sites, the Dome of the Rock. Muslims believe that the prophet Muhammad ascended to Heaven from a slab of stone — the "Rock of Foundation" — located

---

46. Lisa Beyer, "Target: Jerusalem," *Time Magazine*, January 18, 1999.
47. Arabs refer to this site as Haram al-Sharif, which is Arabic for "Noble Sanctuary." Israelis refer to it as Har HaBayit, which is Hebrew for "Temple Mount." American news organizations almost always refer to it as the Temple Mount. Therefore, for the sake of simplicity and continuity, the term Temple Mount will be used in this report when referring to this section of Jerusalem.

in the center of what is now the Dome of the Rock. In addition, when Arab armies conquered Jerusalem in A.D. 638, the Caliph Omar built the al-Aqsa Mosque facing the Dome of the Rock on the opposite end of the Temple Mount. The Western (or Wailing) Wall, the last remnant of the second Jewish temple that the Romans destroyed in A.D. 70, stands at the western base of the Temple Mount. The Western Wall has long been a favorite pilgrimage site for Jews, and religious men and women pray there on a daily basis. Thus, the Temple Mount is equally revered by Jews as the site upon which the first and second Jewish temples stood.

Israeli officials are extremely concerned that the Temple Mount, an area already seething with tension and distrust among Jews and Muslims, will be the stage for violent encounters between religious zealots. Most troubling is the fact that an act of terrorism need not be the catalyst that sparks widespread violence. Indeed, a simple symbolic act of desecration, or even perceived desecration, of any of the holy sites on the Temple Mount is likely to trigger a violent reaction. For example, the Islamic holy month of Ramadan is expected to coincide with the arrival of the year 2000. Thus, even minor provocations on or near the Temple Mount may provide the impetus for a violent confrontation.

The implications of pilgrimages to Jerusalem by vast numbers of tourists are ominous, particularly since such pilgrimages are likely to include millennial or apocalyptic cults on a mission to hasten the arrival of the Messiah. There is general concern among Israeli officials that Jewish and Islamic extremists may react violently to the influx of Christians, particularly near the Temple Mount. The primary concern is that extreme millennial cults will engage in proactive violence designed to hasten the second coming of Christ. Perhaps the most likely scenario involves an attack on the Al-Aqsa Mosque or the Dome of the Rock. Some millennial cults hold that these structures must be destroyed so that the Jewish Temple can be rebuilt, which they see as a prerequisite for the return of the Messiah. Additionally, several religious cults have already made inroads into Israel, apparently in preparation for what they believe to be the endtimes.

It is beyond the scope of this document to assess the potential repercussions from an attack on Jewish or Islamic holy sites in Jerusalem. It goes without saying, however, that an attack on the Dome of the Rock or the Al-Aqsa Mosque would have serious implications. In segments of the Islamic world, close political and cultural ties between Israel and the United States are often perceived as symbolic of anti-Islamic policies by the Western world. Attacks on Islamic holy sites in Jerusalem, particularly by Christian or Jewish extremists, are likely to be perceived by Islamic extremists as attacks on Islam itself. Finally, the possibility exists that Islamic extremist groups will capitalize upon the huge influx of foreigners into Jerusalem and engage in a symbolic attack.

IX. CONCLUSION

Extremists from various ideological perspectives attach significance to the arrival of the year 2000, and there are some signs of preparation for violence. The significance of the new millennium is based primarily upon either religious beliefs relating to the Apocalypse/Armageddon, or political beliefs relating to the New World Order conspiracy theory. The challenge to law enforcement is to understand these extremist theories and, if any incidents do occur, be prepared to respond to the unique crises they will represent.

Law enforcement officials should be particularly aware that the new millennium may increase the odds that extremists may engage in proactive violence specifically targeting law enforcement officers. Religiously motivated extremists may initiate violent conflicts with law enforcement officials in an attempt to facilitate the onset of Armageddon, or to help fulfill a "prophecy." For many on the extreme right-wing, the battle of Armageddon is interpreted as a race war to be fought between Aryans and the "satanic" Jews and their allies. Likewise, extremists who are convinced that the millennium will lead to a One World Government may choose to engage in violence to prevent such a situation from occurring. In either case, extremists motivated by the milllennium could choose martyrdom when approached or confronted by law enforcement officers. Thus, law enforcement officials should be alert for the following: 1) plans to initiate conflict with law enforcement; 2) the potential increase in the number of extremists willing to become martyrs; and 3) the potential for a quicker escalation of conflict during routine law enforcement activities (e.g. traffic stops, issuance of warrants, etc.).

Document B

Earth Charter

PREAMBLE

In our diverse yet increasingly interdependent world, it is imperative that we, the people of Earth, declare our responsibility to one another, to the greater community of life, and to future generations. We are one human family and one Earth community with a common destiny.

Humanity is part of a vast evolving universe. Earth, our home, is alive with a unique community of life. The well-being of people and the biosphere depends upon preserving clean air, pure waters, fertile soils, and a rich variety of plants, animals, and ecosystems. The global environment with its finite resources is a primary common concern of all humanity. The protection of Earth's vitality, diversity, and beauty is a sacred trust.

The Earth community stands at a defining moment. With science and technology have come great benefits and also great harm. The dominant patterns of production and consumption are altering climate, degrading the environment, depleting resources, and causing a massive extinction of species. A dramatic rise in population has increased the pressures on ecological systems and has overburdened social systems. Injustice, poverty, ignorance, corruption, crime and violence, and armed conflict deepen the world's suffering. Fundamental changes in our attitudes, values, and ways of living are necessary.

The choice is ours: to care for Earth and one another or to participate in the destruction of ourselves and the diversity of life.

As a global civilization comes into being, we can choose to build a truly democratic world, securing the rule of law and the human rights of all women, men, and children. We can respect the integrity of different cultures. We can treat Earth with respect, rejecting the idea that nature is merely a collection of resources to be used. We can realize that our social, economic, environmental, and spiritual problems are interconnected and cooperate in developing integrated strategies to address them. We can resolve to balance and harmonize individual interests with the common good, freedom with responsibility, diversity with unity, short term objectives with long term goals, economic progress with the flourishing of ecological systems.

To fulfill these aspirations, we must recognize that human development is not just about having more, but also about being more. The challenges humanity faces can only be met if people everywhere acquire an awareness of global interdependence, identify themselves with the larger world, and decide to live with a sense of universal responsibility. The spirit of human solidarity and kinship with all life will be strengthened if we live with reverence for the sources of our being, gratitude for the gift of life, and humility regarding the human place in the larger scheme of things.

Having reflected on these considerations, we recognize the urgent need for a shared vision of basic values that will provide an ethical foundation for the emerging world community. We, therefore, affirm the following principles for sustainable development. We commit ourselves as individuals, organizations, business enterprises, communities, and nations to implement these interrelated principles and to create a global partnership in support of their fulfillment.

Together in hope, we pledge to:

I. GENERAL PRINCIPLES

1. Respect Earth and all life,
recognizing the interdependence and intrinsic value of all beings;

affirming respect for the inherent dignity of every person and faith in the intellectual, ethical, and spiritual potential of humanity.

2. Care for the community of life in all its diversity

accepting that responsibility for Earth is shared by everyone; affirming that this common responsibility takes different forms for different individuals, groups, and nations, depending on their contribution to existing problems and the resources at hand.

3. Strive to build free, just, participatory, sustainable and peaceful societies,

affirming that with freedom, knowledge, and power goes responsibility and the need for moral self-restraint;

recognizing that a decent standard of living for all and the quality of relations among people and with nature are the true measure of progress.

4. Secure Earth's abundance and beauty for present and future generations,

accepting the challenge before each generation to conserve, improve, and expand their natural and cultural heritage and to transmit it safely to future generations;

acknowledge that the benefits and burdens of caring for Earth should be shared fairly between present and future generations.

II. ECOLOGICAL INTEGRITY

5. Protect and restore the integrity of Earth's ecological systems, with special concern for biological diversity and the natural processes that sustain and renew life.

1. Make ecological conservation an integral part of all development planning and implementation.

2. Establish representative and viable nature and biosphere reserves, including wild lands, sufficient to maintain Earth's biological diversity and life-support systems.

3. Manage the extraction of renewable resources such as food, water, and wood in ways that do not harm the resilience and productivity of ecological systems or threaten the viability of individual species.

4. Promote the recovery of endangered species and populations through in situ conservation involving habitat protection and restoration.

5. Take all reasonable measures to prevent the human-mediated introduction of alien species into the environment.

6. Prevent harm to the environment as the best method of ecological protection and, when knowledge is limited, take the path of caution.

1. Give special attention in decision making to the cumulative, long-term, and global consequences of individual actions.

2. Stop activities that threaten irreversible or serious harm even when scientific information is incomplete or inconclusive.

3. Establish environmental protection standards and monitoring systems with the power to detect significant human environmental impacts, and require environmental impact assessments and reporting.

4. Mandate that the polluter must bear the full cost of pollution.

5. Ensure that measures taken to prevent or control natural disasters, infestations, and diseases are directed to the relevant causes and avoid harmful side effects.

6. Uphold the international obligation of states to take all reasonable precautionary measure to prevent transboundary environmental harm.

7. Treat all living beings with compassion, and protect them from cruelty and wanton destruction.

III. A JUST AND SUSTAINABLE ECONOMIC ORDER

8. Adopt patterns of consumption, production, and reproduction that respect and safeguard Earth's regenerative capacities, human rights, and community well-being.

1. Eliminate harmful waste, and work to ensure that all waste can be either consumed by biological systems or used over the long-term in industrial and technological systems.
2. Act with restraint and efficiency when using energy and other resources, and reduce, reuse, and recycle materials.
3. Rely increasingly on renewable energy sources such as the sun, the wind, biomass, and hydrogen.
4. Establish market prices and economic indicators that reflect the full environmental and social costs of human activities, taking into account the economic value of the services provided by ecological systems.
5. Empower consumers to choose sustainable products over unsustainable ones by creating mechanisms such as certification and labeling.
6. Provide universal access to health care that fosters reproductive health and responsible reproduction.

9. Ensure that economic activities support and promote human development in an equitable and sustainable manner.

1. Promote the equitable distribution of wealth.
2. Assist all communities and nations in developing the intellectual, financial, and technical resources to meet their basic needs, protect the environment, and improve the quality of life.

10. Eradicate poverty, as an ethical, social, economic, and ecological imperative.

1. Establish fair and just access to land, natural resources, train-

ing, knowledge, and credit, empowering every person to attain a secure and sustainable livelihood.

2. Generate opportunities for productive and meaningful employment.
3. Make clean affordable energy available to all.
4. Recognize the ignored, protect the vulnerable, serve those who suffer, and respect their right to develop their capacities and to pursue their aspirations.
5. Relieve developing nations of onerous international debts that impede their progress in meeting basic human needs through sustainable development.

11. Honor and defend the right of all persons, without discrimination, to an environment supportive of their dignity, bodily health, and spiritual well-being.

1. Secure the human right to potable water, clean air, uncontaminated soil, food security, and safe sanitation in urban, rural, and remote environments.
2. Establish racial, religious, ethnic, and socioeconomic equality.
3. Affirm the right of indigenous peoples to their spirituality, knowledge, lands, and resources and to their related practice of traditional sustainable livelihoods.
4. Institute effective and efficient access to administrative and judicial procedures, including redress and remedy, that enable all persons to enforce their environmental rights.

12. Advance worldwide the cooperative study of ecological systems, the dissemination and application of knowledge, and the development, adoption, and transfer of clean technologies.

1. Support scientific research in the public interest.
2. Value the traditional knowledge of indigenous peoples and local communities.
3. Assess and regulate emerging technologies, such as biotech-

nology, regarding their environmental, health, and socioeconomic impacts.

4. Ensure that the exploration and use of orbital and outer space supports peace and sustainable development.

IV. DEMOCRACY AND PEACE

13. Establish access to information, inclusive participation in decision making, and transparency, truthfulness, and accountability in governance.

1. Secure the right of all persons to be informed about ecological, economic, and social developments that affect the quality of their lives.
2. Establish and protect the freedom of association and the right to dissent on matters of environmental, economic, and social policy.
3. Ensure that knowledge resources vital to people's basic needs and development remain accessible and in the public domain.
4. Enable local communities to care for their own environments, and assign responsibilities for environmental protection to the levels of government where they can be carried out most effectively.
5. Create mechanisms that hold governments, international organizations, and business enterprises accountable to the public for the consequences of their activities.

14. Affirm and promote gender equality as a prerequisite to sustainable development.

1. Provide, on the basis of gender equality, universal access to education, health care, and employment in order to support the full development of every person's human dignity and potential.
2. Establish the full and equal participation of women in civil, cultural, economic, political, and social life.

15. **Make the knowledge, values, and skills needed to build just and sustainable communities an integral part of formal education and lifelong learning for all.**
    1. Provide youth with the training and resources required to participate effectively in civil society and political affairs.
    2. Encourage the contribution of the artistic imagination and the humanities as well as the sciences in environmental education and sustainable development.
    3. Engage the media in the challenge for fully educating the public on sustainable development, and take advantage of the educational opportunities provided by advanced information technologies.

16. **Create a culture of peace and cooperation.**
    1. Seek wisdom and inner peace.
    2. Practice nonviolence, implement comprehensive strategies to prevent violent conflict, and use collaborative problem solving to manage and resolve conflict.
    3. Teach tolerance and forgiveness, and promote cross cultural and interreligious dialogue and collaboration.
    4. Eliminate weapons of mass destruction, promote disarmament, secure the environment against severe damage caused by military activities, and convert military resources toward peaceful purposes.
    5. Recognize that peace is the wholeness created by balanced and harmonious relationships with oneself, other persons, other cultures, other life, Earth, and the larger whole of which all are a part.

A New Beginning

As never before in human history, common destiny beckons us to redefine our priorities and to seek a new beginning. Such renewal is the promise of these Earth Charter principles, which are the outcome of a worldwide dialogue in search of common ground and shared values. Fulfillment of this promise depends upon our expanding and deepening the global dialogue. It requires an inner change — a change of heart and mind. It requires that we take decisive action to adopt, apply and develop the vision of the Earth Charter locally, nationally, regionally, and globally. Different cultures and communities will find their own distinctive ways to express the vision, and we will have much to learn from each other.

Every individual, family, organization, corporation, and government has a critical role to play. Youth are fundamental actors for change. Partnerships must be forged at all levels. Our best thought and action will flow from the integration of knowledge with love and compassion.

In order to build a sustainable global community, the nations of the world must renew their commitment to the United Nations and develop and implement the Earth Charter principles by negotiating for adoption a binding agreement based on the IUCN Draft International Covenant on Environment and Development. Adoption of the Covenant will provide an integrated legal framework for environmental and sustainable development and law policy.

We can, if we will take advantage of the creative possibilities before us and inaugurate an era of fresh hope. Let ours be a time that is remembered for an awakening to a new reverence for life, a firm commitment to restoration of Earth's ecological integrity, a quickening of the struggle for justice and empowerment of the people, cooperative engagement of global problems, peaceful management of change, and joyful celebration of life. We will succeed because we must.

Executive Order 12919

National Defense Industrial Resources Preparedness

By the authority vested in me as President by the Constitution and the laws of the United States of America, including the Defense Production Act of 1950, as amended (64 Stat. 798; 50 U.S.C. App. 2061, et seq.), and section 301 of title 3, United States Code, and as Commander in Chief of the Armed Forces of the United States, it is hereby ordered as follows:

Part I — Purpose, Policy and Implementation

Section 101. *Purpose.* This order delegates authorities and addresses national defense industrial resource policies and programs under the Defense Production Act of 1950, as amended ("the Act"), except for the amendments to Title III of the Act in the Energy Security Act of 1980 and telecommunication authorities under Executive Order No. 12472.

Section 102. *Policy.* The United States must have an industrial and technology base capable of meeting national defense requirements, and capable of contributing to the technological superiority of its defense equipment in peacetime and in times of national emergency. The domestic industrial and technological base is the foundation for national defense preparedness. The authorities provided in the Act shall be used to strengthen this base and to ensure it is capable of responding to all threats to the national security of the United States.

Section 103. *General Functions.* Federal departments and agencies responsible for defense acquisition (or for industrial resources needed to support defense acquisition) shall:

a. Identify requirements for the full spectrum of national security emergencies, including military, industrial, and essential civilian demand;

b. Assess continually the capability of the domestic industrial and technological base to satisfy requirements in peacetime and times of national emergency, specifically evaluating the availability of adequate industrial resource and production sources, including subcontractors and suppliers, materials, skilled labor, and professional and technical personnel;

c. Be prepared, in the event of a potential threat to the security of the United States, to take actions necessary to ensure the availability of adequate industrial resources and production capability, including services and critical technology for national defense requirements;

d. Improve the efficiency and responsiveness, to defense requirements, of the domestic industrial base; and

e. Foster cooperation between the defense and commercial sectors for research and development and for acquisition of materials, components, and equipment to enhance industrial base efficiency and responsiveness.

Section 104. *Implementation.*

a. The National Security Council is the principal forum for consideration and resolution of national security resource preparedness policy.

b. The Director, Federal Emergency Management Agency ("Director, FEMA") shall:

1. Serve as an advisor to the National Security Council on issues of national security resource preparedness and on the use of the authorities and functions delegated by this order;

2. Provide for the central coordination of the plans and programs incident to authorities and functions delegated under this order, and provide guidance and procedures approved by the Assistant to the President for National Security Affairs to the Federal departments and agencies under this

order;

3. Establish procedures, in consultation with Federal departments and agencies assigned functions under this order, to resolve in a timely and effective manner conflicts and issues that may arise in implementing the authorities and functions delegated under this order; and

4. Report to the President periodically concerning all program activities conducted pursuant to this order.

c. The head of every Federal department and agency assigned functions under this order shall ensure that the performance of these functions is consistent with National Security Council policy and guidelines.

Part II — Priorities and Allocations

Section 201. *Delegations of Priorities and Allocations.*

a. The authority of the President conferred by section 101 of the Act to require acceptance and priority performance of contracts or orders (other than contracts of employment) to promote the national defense over performance of any other contracts or orders, and to allocate materials, services, and facilities as deemed necessary or appropriate to promote the national defense, is delegated to the following agency heads:

1. The Secretary of Agriculture with respect to food resources, food resource facilities, and the domestic distribution of farm equipment and commercial fertilizer;

2. The Secretary of Energy with respect to all forms of energy;

3. The Secretary of Health and Human Services with respect to health resources;

4. The Secretary of Transportation with respect to all forms of civil transportation;

5. The Secretary of Defense with respect to water resources; and

6. The Secretary of Commerce for all other materials, services, and facilities, including construction materials.

b. The Secretary of Commerce, in consultation with the heads of
those departments and agencies specified in subsection 201(a)
of this order, shall administer the Defense Priorities and Allocations System ("DPAS") regulations that will be used to implement the authority of the President conferred by section
101 of the Act as delegated to the Secretary of Commerce in
subsection 201(a)(6) of this order. The Secretary of Commerce
will redelegate to the Secretary of Defense, and the heads of
other departments and agencies as appropriate, authority for
the priority rating of contracts and orders for all materials,
services, and facilities needed in support of programs approved
under section 202 of this order. The Secretary of Commerce
shall act as appropriate upon Special Priorities Assistance requests in a time frame consistent with the urgency of the need
at hand.

c. The Director, FEMA, shall attempt to resolve issues or disagree-
ments on priorities or allocations between Federal departments
or agencies in a time frame consistent with the urgency of the
issue at hand and, if not resolved, such issues will be referred
to the Assistant to the President for National Security Affairs
for final determination.

d. The head of each Federal department or agency assigned functions under subsection 201(a) of this order, when necessary,
shall make the finding required under subsection 101(b) of the
Act. This finding shall be submitted for the President's approval through the Assistant to the President for National Security Affairs. Upon such approval the head of the Federal
department or agency that made the finding may use the authority of subsection 101(a) of the Act to control the general
distribution of any material (including applicable services) in
the civilian market.

e. The Assistant to the President for National Security Affairs is
hereby delegated the authority under subsection 101(c)(3) of
the Act, and will be assisted by the Director, FEMA, in ensur-

ing the coordinated administration of the Act.

Section 202. *Determinations.* The authority delegated by section 201 of this order may be used only to support programs that have been determined in writing as necessary or appropriate to promote the national defense:

a. By the Secretary of Defense with respect to military production and construction, military assistance to foreign nations, stockpiling, outer space, and directly related activities;

b. By the Secretary of Energy with respect to energy production and construction, distribution and use, and directly related activities; and

c. By the Director, FEMA, with respect to essential civilian needs supporting national defense, including civil defense and continuity of government and directly related activities.

Section 203. *Maximizing Domestic Energy Supplies.* The authority of the President to perform the functions provided by subsection 101(c) of the Act is delegated to the Secretary of Commerce, who shall redelegate to the Secretary of Energy the authority to make the findings described in subsection 101(c)(2)(A) that the materials (including equipment), services, and facilities are critical and essential. The Secretary of Commerce shall make the finding described in subsection 101(c)(2)(A) of the Act that the materials (including equipment), services, or facilities are scarce, and the finding described in subsection 101(c)(2)(B) that it is necessary to use the authority provided by subsection 101(c)(1).

Section 204. *Chemical and Biological Warfare.* The authority of the President conferred by subsection 104(b) of the Act is delegated to the Secretary of Defense. This authority may not be further delegated by the Secretary.

Part III — Expansion of Productive Capacity and Supply
Section 301.

a. *Financing Institution Guarantees.* To expedite or expand production and deliveries or services under government contracts for the procurement of industrial resources or critical technology items essential to the national defense, the head of each Federal department or agency engaged in procurement for the national defense (referred to as "agency head" in this part) and the President and Chairman of the Export-Import Bank of the United States (in cases involving capacity expansion, technological development, or production in foreign countries) are authorized to guarantee in whole or in part any public or private financing institution, subject to provisions of section 301 of the Act. Guarantees shall be made in consultation with the Department of the Treasury as to the terms and conditions thereof. The Director of the Office of Management and Budget ("OMB") shall be informed when such guarantees are to be made.

b. *Direct Loan Guarantees.* To expedite or expand production and deliveries or services under government contracts for the procurement of industrial resources or critical technology items essential to the national defense, each agency head is authorized to make direct loan guarantees from funds appropriated to their agency for Title III.

c. *Fiscal Agent.* Each Federal Reserve Bank is designated and authorized to act, on behalf of any guaranteeing agency, as fiscal agent in the making of guarantee contracts and in otherwise carrying out the purposes of section 301 of the Act.

d. *Regulations.* The Board of Governors of the Federal Reserve System is authorized, after consultation with heads of guaranteeing departments and agencies, the Secretary of the Treasury, and the Director, OMB, to prescribe regulations governing procedures, forms, rates of interest, and fees for such guarantee contracts.

Section 302. *Loans.*

a. To expedite production and deliveries or services to aid in carrying out government contracts for the procurement of industrial resources or a critical technology item for the national defense, an agency head is authorized, subject to the provisions of section 302 of the Act, to submit to the Secretary of the Treasury or the President and Chairman of the Export-Import Bank of the United States (in cases involving capacity expansion, technological development, or production in foreign countries) applications for loans.

b. To expedite or expand production and deliveries or services under government contracts for the procurement of industrial resources or critical technology items essential to the national defense, each agency head may make direct loans from funds appropriated to their agency for Title III.

c. After receiving a loan application and determining that financial assistance is not otherwise available on reasonable terms, the Secretary of the Treasury or the President and Chairman of the Export-Import Bank of the United States (in cases involving capacity expansion, technological development, or production in foreign countries) may make loans, subject to provisions of section 302 of the Act.

Section 303. *Purchase Commitments.*

a. In order to carry out the objectives of the Act, and subject to the provisions of section 303 thereof, an agency head is authorized to make provision for purchases of, or commitments to purchase, an industrial resource or a critical technology item for government use or resale.

b. Materials acquired under section 303 of the Act that exceed the needs of the programs under the Act may be transferred to the National Defense Stockpile, if such transfer is determined by the Secretary of Defense as the National Defense Stockpile Manager to be in the public interest.

Section 304. *Subsidy Payments.* In order to ensure the supply of raw or non-processed materials from high-cost sources, an agency head is authorized to make subsidy payments, after consultation with the Secretary of the Treasury and the Director, OMB, and subject to the provisions of section 303(c) of the Act.

Section 305. *Determinations and Findings.* When carrying out the authorities in sections 301 through 303 of this order, an agency head is authorized to make the required determinations, judgments, statements, certifications, and findings, in consultation with the Secretary of Defense, Secretary of Energy or Director, FEMA, as appropriate. The agency head shall provide a copy of the determination, judgment, statement, certification, or finding to the Director, OMB, to the Director, FEMA, and, when appropriate, to the Secretary of the Treasury.

Section 306. *Strategic and Critical Materials.*

a. The Secretary of the Interior, in consultation with the Secretary of Defense as the National Defense Stockpile Manager and subject to the provisions of section 303 of the Act, is authorized to encourage the exploration, development, and mining of critical and strategic materials and other materials.

b. An agency head is authorized, pursuant to section 303(g) of the Act, to make provision for the development of substitutes for strategic and critical materials, critical components, critical technology items, and other industrial resources to aid the national defense.

c. An agency head is authorized, pursuant to section 303(a)(1)(B) of the Act, to make provisions to encourage the exploration, development, and mining of critical and strategic materials and other materials.

Section 307. *Government-owned Equipment.* An agency head is authorized, pursuant to section 303(e) of the Act, to install additional equipment, facilities, processes, or improvements to facilities owned by the government and to install government-owned equipment in industrial facilities owned by private persons.

Section 308. *Identification of Shortfalls.* Except during periods of national emergency or after a Presidential determination in accordance with sections 301(e) (1)(D)(ii), 302(c)(4)(B), or 303(a)(7)(B) of the Act, no guarantee, loan or other action pursuant to sections 301, 302, and 303 of the Act to correct an industrial shortfall shall be taken unless the shortfall has been identified in the Budget of the United States or amendments thereto.

Section 309. *Defense Production Act Fund Manager.* The Secretary of Defense is designated the Defense Production Act Fund Manager, in accordance with section 304(f) of the Act, and shall carry out the duties specified in that section, in consultation with the agency heads having approved Title III projects and appropriated Title III funds.

Section 310. *Critical Items List.*

a. Pursuant to section 107(b)(1)(A) of the Act, the Secretary of Defense shall identify critical components and critical technology items for each item on the Critical Items List of the Commanders-in-Chief of the Unified and Specified Commands and other items within the inventory of weapon systems and defense equipment.

b. Each agency head shall take appropriate action to ensure that critical components or critical technology items are available from reliable sources when needed to meet defense requirements during peacetime, graduated mobilization, and national emergency. "Appropriate action" may include restricting contract solicitations to reliable sources, restricting contract solicitations to domestic sources (pursuant to statutory authority), stockpiling critical components, and developing substitutes for critical components or critical technology items.

Section 311. *Strengthening Domestic Capability.* An agency head, in accordance with section 107(a) of the Act, may utilize the authority of Title III of the Act or any other provision of law, in consultation with the Secretary of Defense, to provide appropriate incentives to develop, maintain, modernize, and expand the productive capacities of domestic sources for critical components, critical technology items, and industrial resources essential for the execution of the national security strategy of the United States.

Section 312. *Modernization of Equipment.* An agency head, in accordance with section 108(b) of the Act, may utilize the authority of Title III of the Act to guarantee the purchase or lease of advance manufacturing equipment and any related services with respect to any such equipment for purposes of the Act.

Part IV — Impact of Offsets

Section 401. *Offsets.*

a. The responsibilities and authority conferred upon the President by section 309 of the Act with respect to offsets are delegated to the Secretary of Commerce, who shall function as the President's Executive Agent for carrying out this authority.

b. The Secretary of Commerce shall prepare the annual report required by section 309(a) of the Act in consultation with the Secretaries of Defense, Treasury, Labor, State, the United States Trade Representative, the Arms Control and Disarmament Agency, the Director of Central Intelligence, and the heads of other departments and agencies as required. The heads of Federal departments and agencies shall provide the Secretary of Commerce with such information as may be necessary for the effective performance of this function.

c. The offset report shall be subject to the normal interagency clearance process conducted by the Director, OMB, prior to the report's submission by the President to Congress.

Part V — Voluntary Agreements and Advisory Committees

Section 501. *Appointments.* The authority of the President under sections 708(c) and (d) of the Act is delegated to the heads of each Federal department or agency, except that, insofar as that authority relates to section 101 of the Act, it is delegated only to the heads of each Federal department or agency assigned functions under section 201(a) of this order. The authority delegated under this section shall be exercised pursuant to the provisions of section 708 of the Act, and copies and the status of the use of such delegations shall be furnished to the Director, FEMA.

Section 502. *Advisory Committees.* The authority of the President under section 708(d) of the Act and delegated in section 501 of this order (relating to establishment of advisory committees) shall be exercised only after consultation with, and in accordance with, guidelines and procedures established by the Administrator of General Services.

Part VI — Employment of Personnel

Section 601. *National Defense Executive Reserve.*

a. In accordance with section 710(e) of the Act, there is established in the Executive Branch a National Defense Executive Reserve ("NDER") composed of persons of recognized expertise from various segments of the private sector and from government (except full-time federal employees) for training for employment in executive positions in the Federal Government in the event of an emergency that requires such employment.

b. The head of any department or agency may establish a unit of the NDER in the department or agency and train members of that unit.

c. The head of each department or agency with an NDER unit is authorized to exercise the President's authority to employ civilian personnel in accordance with section 703(a) of the Act when activating all or a part of its NDER unit. The exercise of this authority shall be subject to the provisions of subsections 601(d) and (e) of this order and shall not be redelegated.

d. The head of a department or agency may activate an NDER unit, in whole or in part, upon the written determination that an emergency affecting the national security or defense preparedness of the United States exists and that the activation of the unit is necessary to carry out the emergency program functions of the department or agency.

e. At least 72 hours prior to activating the NDER unit, the head of the department or agency shall notify, in writing, the Assistant to the President for National Security Affairs of the impending activation and provide a copy of the determination required under subsection 601(d) of this order.

f. The Director, FEMA, shall coordinate the NDER program activities of departments and agencies in establishing units of the Reserve; provide for appropriate guidance for recruitment, training, and activation; and issue necessary rules and guidance in connection with the program.

g. This order suspends any delegated authority, regulation, or other requirement or condition with respect to the activation of any NDER unit, in whole or in part, or appointment of any NDER member that is inconsistent with the authorities delegated herein, provided that the aforesaid suspension applies only as long as sections 703(a) and 710(e) of the Act are in effect.

Section 602. *Consultants.* The head of each department or agency assigned functions under this order is delegated authority under sections 710(b) and (c) of the Act to employ persons of outstanding experience and ability without compensation and to employ experts, consultants, or organizations. The authority delegated by this section shall not be redelegated.

Part VII — Labor Supply

Section 701. *Secretary of Labor.* The Secretary of Labor, identified in this section as the Secretary, shall:

a. Collect, analyze, and maintain data needed to make a continuing appraisal of the nation's labor requirements and the supply of workers for purposes of national defense. All agencies of the government shall cooperate with the Secretary in furnishing information necessary for this purpose, to the extent permitted by law;

b. In response to requests from the head of a Federal department or agency engaged in the procurement for national defense, consult with and advise that department or agency with respect to (1) the effect of contemplated actions on labor supply and utilization, (2) the relation of labor supply to materials and facilities requirements, and (3) such other matters as will assist in making the exercise of priority and allocations functions consistent with effective utilization and distribution of labor;

c. Formulate plans, programs, and policies for meeting defense and essential civilian labor requirements;

d. Project skill shortages to facilitate meeting defense and essential civilian needs and establish training programs;

e. Determine the occupations and skills critical to meeting the labor requirements of defense and essential civilian activities and, with the assistance of the Secretary of Defense, the Director of Selective Service, and such other persons as the Director, FEMA, may designate, develop policies regulating the induction and deferment of personnel for the armed services, except for civilian personnel in the reserves; and

f. Administer an effective labor-management relations policy to support the activities and programs under this order with the cooperation of other Federal agencies, including the National Labor Relations Board and the Federal Mediation and Conciliation Service.

Part VIII — Defense Industrial Base
Information and Reports

Section 801. *Foreign Acquisition of Companies.* The Secretary of the Treasury, in cooperation with the Department of State, the Department of Defense, the Department of Commerce, the Department of Energy, the Department of Agriculture, the Attorney General, and the Director of Central Intelligence, shall complete and furnish a report to the President and then to Congress in accordance with the requirements of section 721(k) of the Act concerning foreign efforts to acquire United States companies involved in research, development, or production of critical technologies and industrial espionage activities directed by foreign governments against private U.S. companies.

Section 802. *Defense Industrial Base Information System.*

a. The Secretary of Defense and the heads of other appropriate Federal departments and agencies, as determined by the Secretary of Defense, shall establish an information system on the domestic defense industrial base in accordance with the requirements of section 722 of the Act.

b. In establishing the information system required by subsection (a) of this order, the Secretary of Defense, the Secretary of Commerce, and the heads of other appropriate Federal departments and agencies, as determined by the Secretary of Defense in consultation with the Secretary of Commerce, shall consult with each other for the purposes of performing the duties listed in section 722(d)(1) of the Act.

c. The Secretary of Defense shall convene a task force consisting of the Secretary of Commerce and the Secretary of each military department and the heads of other appropriate Federal departments and agencies, as determined by the Secretary of Defense in consultation with the Secretary of Commerce, to carry out the duties under section 722(d)(2) of the Act.

d. The Secretary of Defense shall report to Congress on a strategic plan for developing a cost-effective, comprehensive information system capable of identifying on a timely, ongoing basis vulnerability in critical components and critical technology items. The plans shall include an assessment of the performance and cost-effectiveness of procedures specified in section 722(b) of the Act.

e. The Secretary of Commerce, acting through the Bureau of the Census, shall consult with the Secretary of Defense and the Director, FEMA, to improve the usefulness of information derived from the Census of Manufacturers in carrying out section 722 of the Act.

f. The Secretary of Defense shall perform an analysis of the production base for not more than two major weapons systems of each military department in establishing the information system under section 722 of the Act. Each analysis shall identify the critical components of each system.

g. The Secretary of Defense, in consultation with the Secretary of Commerce, and the heads of other Federal departments and agencies as appropriate, shall issue a biennial report on critical components and technology in accordance with section 722(e) of the Act.

Part IX — General Provisions

Section 901. *Definitions.* In addition to the definitions in section 702 of the Act, the following definitions apply throughout this order:

a. "Civil transportation" includes movement of persons and property by all modes of transportation in interstate, intrastate, or foreign commerce within the United States, its territories and possessions, and the District of Columbia, and, without limitation, related public storage and warehousing, ports, services, equipment and facilities, such as transportation carrier shop and repair facilities. However, "civil transportation" shall not include transportation owned or controlled by the Department of Defense, use of petroleum and gas pipelines, and coal slurry pipelines used only to supply energy production facilities directly. As applied herein, "civil transportation" shall include direction, control, and coordination of civil transportation capacity regardless of ownership.

b. "Energy" means all forms of energy including petroleum, gas (both natural and manufactured), electricity, solid fuels (including all forms of coal, coke, coal chemicals, coal liquification, and coal gasification), and atomic energy, and the production, conservation, use, control, and distribution (including pipelines) of all of these forms of energy.

c. "Farm equipment" means equipment, machinery, and repair

parts manufactured for use on farms in connection with the production or preparation for market use of food resources.

d. "Fertilizer" means any product or combination of products that contain one or more of the elements — nitrogen, phosphorus, and potassium — for use as a plant nutrient.

e. "Food resources" means all commodities and products, simple, mixed, or compound, or complements to such commodities or products, that are capable of being ingested by either human beings or animals, irrespective of other uses to which such commodities or products may be put, at all stages of processing from the raw commodity to the products thereof in vendible form for human or animal consumption. "Food resources" also means all starches, sugars, vegetable and animal or marine fats and oils, cotton, tobacco, wool, mohair, hemp, flax fiber, and naval stores, but does not mean any such material after it loses its identity as an agricultural commodity or agricultural product.

f. "Food resource facilities" means plants, machinery, vehicles (including on-farm), and other facilities required for the production, processing, distribution, and storage (including cold storage) of food resources, livestock and poultry feed and seed, and for the domestic distribution of farm equipment and fertilizer (excluding transportation thereof).

g. "Functions" include powers, duties, authority, responsibilities, and discretion.

h. "Head of each Federal department or agency engaged in procurement for the national defense" means the heads of the Departments of Defense, Energy, and Commerce, as well as those departments and agencies listed in Executive Order No. 10789.

i, "Heads of other appropriate Federal departments and agencies" as used in part VIII of this order means the heads of such other Federal agencies and departments that acquire information or need information with respect to making any determination to exercise any authority under the Act.

j. "Health resources" means materials, facilities, health supplies, and equipment (including pharmaceutical, blood collecting and dispensing supplies, biological, surgical textiles, and emergency surgical instruments and supplies) required to prevent the impairment of, improve, or restore the physical and mental health conditions of the population.

k. "Metals and minerals" means all raw materials of mineral origin (excluding energy) including their refining, smelting, or processing, but excluding their fabrication.

l. "Strategic and Critical Materials" means materials (including energy) that (1) would be needed to supply the military, industrial, and essential civilian needs of the United States during a national security emergency, and (2) are not found or produced in the United States in sufficient quantities to meet such need and are vulnerable to the termination or reduction of the availability of the material.

m. "Water resources" means all usable water, from all sources, within the jurisdiction of the United States, which can be managed, controlled, and allocated to meet emergency requirements.

Section 902. *General.*

a. Except as otherwise provided in subsection 902(c) of this order, the authorities vested in the President by title VII of the Act may be exercised and performed by the head of each department and agency in carrying out the delegated authorities under the Act and this order.

b. The authorities which may be exercised and performed pursuant to subsection 902(a) of this order shall include (1) the power to redelegate authorities, and to authorize the successive redelegation of authorities, to departments and agencies, officers, and employees of the government, and (2) the power of subpoena with respect to authorities delegated in parts II, III, and IV of this order, provided that the subpoena power shall be utilized only after the scope and purpose of the investigation, inspection, or inquiry to which the subpoena relates have been defined either by the appropriate officer identified in subsection 902(a) of this order or by such other person or persons as the officer shall designate.

c. Excluded from the authorities delegated by subsection 902(a) of this order are authorities delegated by parts V, VI, and VIII of this order and the authority with respect to fixing compensation under section 703(a) of the Act.

Section 903. *Authority.* All previously issued orders, regulations, rulings, certificates, directives, and other actions relating to any function affected by this order shall remain in effect except as they are inconsistent with this order or are subsequently amended or revoked under proper authority. Nothing in this order shall affect the validity or force of anything done under previous delegations or other assignment of authority under the Act.

Section 904. *Effect on other Orders.*

a. The following are superseded or revoked:

1. Section 3, Executive Order No. 8248 of September 8, 1939, (4 FR 3864).

2. Executive Order No. 10222 of March 8, 1951 (16 FR 2247).

3. Executive Order No. 10480 of August 14, 1953 (18 FR 4939).

4. Executive Order No. 10647 of November 28, 1955 (20 FR 8769).

5. Executive Order No. 11179 of September 22, 1964 (29 FR 13239).

6. Executive Order No. 11355 of May 26, 1967 (32 FR 7803).

7. Sections 7 and 8, Executive Order No. 11912 of April 13, 1976 (41 FR 15825, 15826-27).

8. Section 3, Executive Order No. 12148 of July 20, 1979 (44 FR 43239, 43241).

9. Executive Order No. 12521 of June 24, 1985 (50 FR 26335).

10. Executive Order No. 12649 of August 11, 1988 (53 FR 30639).

11. Executive Order No. 12773 of September 26, 1991 (56 FR 49387), except that part of the order that amends section 604 of Executive Order 10480.

b. Executive Order No. 10789 of November 14, 1958, is amended by deleting "and in view of the existing national emergency declared by Proclamation No. 2914 of December 16, 1950," as it appears in the first sentence.

c. Executive Order No. 11790, as amended, relating to the Federal Energy Administration Act of 1974, is amended by deleting "Executive Order No. 10480" where it appears in section 4 and substituting this order's number.

d. Subject to subsection 904(c) of this order, to the extent that any provision of any prior Executive order is inconsistent with the provisions of this order, this order shall control and such prior provision is amended accordingly.

Section 905. *Judicial Review.* This order is not intended to create any right or benefit, substantive or procedural, enforceable at law by a party against the United States, its agencies, its officers, or any person.

WILLIAM J. CLINTON

THE WHITE HOUSE,
June 3, 1994

Charter of the United Nations and Statute of the International Court of Justice

Introductory Note

The Charter of the United Nations was signed on 26 June 1945, in San Francisco, at the conclusion of the United Nations Conference on International Organization, and came into force on 24 October 1945. The Statute of the International Court of Justice is an integral part of the Charter.

Amendments to Articles 23, 27 and 61 of the Charter were adopted by the General Assembly on 17 December 1963 and came into force on 31 August 1965. A further amendment to Article 61 was adopted by the General Assembly on 20 December 1971, and came into force on 24 September 1973. An amendment to Article 109, adopted by the General Assembly on 20 December 1965, came into force on 12 June 1968.

The amendment to Article 23 enlarges the membership of the Security Council from eleven to fifteen. The amended Article 27 provides that decisions of the Security Council on procedural matters shall be made by an affirmative vote of nine members (formerly seven) and on all other matters by an affirmative vote of nine members (formerly seven), including the concurring votes of the five permanent members of the Security Council.

The amendment to Article 61, which entered into force on 31 August 1965, enlarged the membership of the Economic and Social Council from eighteen to twenty-seven. The subsequent amendment to that Article, which entered into force on 24 September 1973, further increased the membership of the Council from twenty-seven to fifty-four.

The amendment to Article 109, which relates to the first paragraph of that Article, provides that a General Conference of Member States for the purpose of reviewing the Charter may be held at a date and place to be fixed by a two-thirds vote of the members of the General Assembly and by a vote of any nine members (formerly seven) of the Security Council. Paragraph 3 of Article 109, which deals with the consideration of a possible review conference during the tenth regular session of the General Assembly, has been retained in its original form in its reference to a "vote, of any seven members of the Security Council," the paragraph having been acted upon in 1955 by the General Assembly, at its tenth regular session, and by the Security Council.

Preamble to the Charter of the United Nations

WE THE PEOPLES OF THE UNITED NATIONS DETERMINED

to save succeeding generations from the scourge of war, which twice in our lifetime has brought untold sorrow to mankind, and

to reaffirm faith in fundamental human rights, in the dignity and worth of the human person, in the equal rights of men and women and of nations large and small, and

to establish conditions under which justice and respect for the obligations arising from treaties and other sources of international law can be maintained, and

to promote social progress and better standards of life in larger freedom,

AND FOR THESE ENDS

to practice tolerance and live together in peace with one another as good neighbours, and

to unite our strength to maintain international peace and security, and to ensure, by the acceptance of principles and the institution of methods, that armed force shall not be used, save in the common interest, and

to employ international machinery for the promotion of the economic and social advancement of all peoples,

HAVE RESOLVED TO COMBINE OUR EFFORTS TO ACCOMPLISH THESE AIMS

Accordingly, our respective Governments, through representatives assembled in the city of San Francisco, who have exhibited their full powers found to be in good and due form, have agreed to the present Charter of the United Nations and do hereby establish an international organization to be known as the United Nations.

Chapter I   Purposes and Principles

Article 1

The Purposes of the United Nations are:

1. To maintain international peace and security, and to that end: to take effective collective measures for the prevention and removal of threats to the peace, and for the suppression of acts of aggression or other breaches of the peace, and to bring about by peaceful means, and in conformity with the principles of justice and international law, adjustment or settlement of international disputes or situations which might lead to a breach of the peace;

2. To develop friendly relations among nations based on respect for the principle of equal rights and self-determination of peoples, and to take other appropriate measures to strengthen universal peace;

3. To achieve international cooperation in solving international problems of an economic, social, cultural, or humanitarian character, and in promoting and encouraging respect for human rights and for fundamental freedoms for all without distinction as to race, sex, language, or religion; and

4. To be a centre for harmonizing the actions of nations in the attainment of these common ends.

Article 2

The Organization and its Members, in pursuit of the Purposes stated in Article 1, shall act in accordance with the following Principles.

1. The Organization is based on the principle of the sovereign equality of all its Members.

2. All Members, in order to ensure to all of them the rights and benefits resulting from membership, shall fulfill in good faith the obligations assumed by them in accordance with the present Charter.

3. All Members shall settle their international disputes by peaceful means in such a manner that international peace and security, and justice, are not endangered.

4. All Members shall refrain in their international relations from the threat or use of force against the territorial integrity or political independence of any state, or in any other manner inconsistent with the Purposes of the United Nations.

5. All Members shall give the United Nations every assistance in any action it takes in accordance with the present Charter, and shall refrain from giving assistance to any state against which the United Nations is taking preventive or enforcement action.

6. The Organization shall ensure that states which are not Members of the United Nations act in accordance with these Principles so far as may be necessary for the maintenance of international peace and security.

7. Nothing contained in the present Charter shall authorize the United Nations to intervene in matters which are essentially within the domestic jurisdiction of any state or shall require the Members to submit such matters to settlement under the present Charter; but this principle shall not prejudice the application of enforcement measures under Chapter Vll.

Chapter II   Membership

Article 3

The original Members of the United Nations shall be the states which, having participated in the United Nations Conference on International Organization at San Francisco, or having previously signed the Declaration by United Nations of 1 January 1942, sign the present Charter and ratify it in accordance with Article 110.

Article 4

1. Membership in the United Nations is open to all other peace-loving states which accept the obligations contained in the present Charter and, in the judgment of the Organization, are able and willing to carry out these obligations.
2. The admission of any such state to membership in the United Nations will be effected by a decision of the General Assembly upon the recommendation of the Security Council.

Article 5

A Member of the United Nations against which preventive or enforcement action has been taken by the Security Council may be suspended from the exercise of the rights and privileges of membership by the General Assembly upon the recommendation of the Security Council. The exercise of these rights and privileges may be restored by the Security Council.

Article 6

A Member of the United Nations which has persistently violated the Principles contained in the present Charter may be expelled from the Organization by the General Assembly upon the recommendation of the Security Council.

Chapter III   Organs

Article 7

1. There are established as the principal organs of the United Nations: a General Assembly, a Security Council, an Economic and Social Council, a Trusteeship Council, an International Court of Justice, and a Secretariat.

2. Such subsidiary organs as may be found necessary may be established in accordance with the present Charter.

Article 8
The United Nations shall place no restrictions on the eligibility of men and women to participate in any capacity and under conditions of equality in its principal and subsidiary organs.

Chapter IV   The General Assembly
Composition
Article 9
1. The General Assembly shall consist of all the Members of the United Nations.
2. Each Member shall have not more than five representatives in the General Assembly.

Functions and Powers
Article 10
The General Assembly may discuss any questions or any matters within the scope of the present Charter or relating to the powers and functions of any organs provided for in the present Charter, and, except as provided in Article 12, may make recommendations to the Members of the United Nations or to the Security Council or to both on any such questions or matters.

Article 11
1. The General Assembly may consider the general principles of co-operation in the maintenance of international peace and security, including the principles governing disarmament and the regulation of armaments, and may make recommendations with regard to such principles to the Members or to the Security Council or to both.
2. The General Assembly may discuss any questions relating to the maintenance of international peace and security brought before

it by any Member of the United Nations, or by the Security Council, or by a state which is not a Member of the United Nations in accordance with Article 35, paragraph 2, and, except as provided in Article 12, may make recommendations with regard to any such questions to the state or states concerned or to the Security Council or to both. Any such question on which action is necessary shall be referred to the Security Council by the General Assembly either before or after discussion.

3. The General Assembly may call the attention of the Security Council to situations which are likely to endanger international peace and security.

4. The powers of the General Assembly set forth in this Article shall not limit the general scope of Article 10.

Article 12

1. While the Security Council is exercising in respect of any dispute or situation the functions assigned to it in the present Charter, the General Assembly shall not make any recommendation with regard to that dispute or situation unless the Security Council so requests.

2. The Secretary-General, with the consent of the Security Council, shall notify the General Assembly at each session of any matters relative to the maintenance of international peace and security which are being dealt with by the Security Council and shall similarly notify the General Assembly, or the Members of the United Nations if the General Assembly is not in session, immediately the Security Council ceases to deal with such matters.

Article 13

1. The General Assembly shall initiate studies and make recommendations for the purpose of:

   a. promoting international cooperation in the political field and encouraging the progressive development of international law and its codification;

b. promoting international cooperation in the economic, social, cultural, educational, and health fields, and assisting in the realization of human rights and fundamental freedoms for all without distinction as to race, sex, language, or religion.

2. The further responsibilities, functions and powers of the General Assembly with respect to matters mentioned in paragraph 1 (b) above are set forth in Chapters IX and X.

Article 14

Subject to the provisions of Article 12, the General Assembly may recommend measures for the peaceful adjustment of any situation, regardless of origin, which it deems likely to impair the general welfare or friendly relations among nations, including situations resulting from a violation of the provisions of the present Charter setting forth the Purposes and Principles of the United Nations.

Article 15

1. The General Assembly shall receive and consider annual and special reports from the Security Council; these reports shall include an account of the measures that the Security Council has decided upon or taken to maintain international peace and security.
2. The General Assembly shall receive and consider reports from the other organs of the United Nations.

Article 16

The General Assembly shall perform such functions with respect to the international trusteeship system as are assigned to it under Chapters XII and XIII, including the approval of the trusteeship agreements for areas not designated as strategic.

Article 17

1. The General Assembly shall consider and approve the budget of the Organization.
2. The expenses of the Organization shall be borne by the Members

as apportioned by the General Assembly.

3. The General Assembly shall consider and approve any financial and budgetary arrangements with specialized agencies referred to in Article 57 and shall examine the administrative budgets of such specialized agencies with a view to making recommendations to the agencies concerned.

Voting

Article 18

1. Each member of the General Assembly shall have one vote.

2. Decisions of the General Assembly on important questions shall be made by a two-thirds majority of the members present and voting. These questions shall include: recommendations with respect to the maintenance of international peace and security, the election of the non-permanent members of the Security Council, the election of the members of the Economic and Social Council, the election of members of the Trusteeship Council in accordance with paragraph 1 (c) of Article 86, the admission of new Members to the United Nations, the suspension of the rights and privileges of membership, the expulsion of Members, questions relating to the operation of the trusteeship system, and budgetary questions.

3. Decisions on other questions, including the determination of additional categories of questions to be decided by a two-thirds majority, shall be made by a majority of the members present and voting.

Article 19

A Member of the United Nations which is in arrears in the payment of its financial contributions to the Organization shall have no vote in the General Assembly if the amount of its arrears equals or exceeds the amount of the contributions due from it for the preceding two full years. The General Assembly may, nevertheless, permit such a Member to vote if it is satisfied that the failure to pay is due to conditions beyond the control of the Member.

Procedure
Article 20

The General Assembly shall meet in regular annual sessions and in such special sessions as occasion may require. Special sessions shall be convoked by the Secretary-General at the request of the Security Council or of a majority of the Members of the United Nations.

Article 21

The General Assembly shall adopt its own rules of procedure. It shall elect its President for each session.

Article 22

The General Assembly may establish such subsidiary organs as it deems necessary for the performance of its functions.

Chapter V   The Security Council
Composition
Article 23

1. The Security Council shall consist of fifteen Members of the United Nations. The Republic of China, France, the Union of Soviet Socialist Republics, the United Kingdom of Great Britain and Northern Ireland, and the United States of America shall be permanent members of the Security Council. The General Assembly shall elect ten other Members of the United Nations to be non-permanent members of the Security Council, due regard being specially paid, in the first instance to the contribution of Members of the United Nations to the maintenance of international peace and security and to the other purposes of the Organization, and also to equitable geographical distribution.
2. The non-permanent members of the Security Council shall be elected for a term of two years. In the first election of the non-permanent members after the increase of the membership of the Security Council from eleven to fifteen, two of the four additional

members shall be chosen for a term of one year. A retiring member shall not be eligible for immediate re-election.

3. Each member of the Security Council shall have one representative.

Functions and Powers
Article 24

1. In order to ensure prompt and effective action by the United Nations, its Members confer on the Security Council primary responsibility for the maintenance of international peace and security, and agree that in carrying out its duties under this responsibility the Security Council acts on their behalf.

2. In discharging these duties the Security Council shall act in accordance with the Purposes and Principles of the United Nations. The specific powers granted to the Security Council for the discharge of these duties are laid down in Chapters VI, VII, VIII, and XII.

3. The Security Council shall submit annual and, when necessary, special reports to the General Assembly for its consideration.

Article 25

The Members of the United Nations agree to accept and carry out the decisions of the Security Council in accordance with the present Charter.

Article 26

In order to promote the establishment and maintenance of international peace and security with the least diversion for armaments of the world's human and economic resources, the Security Council shall be responsible for formulating, with the assistance of the Military Staff Committee referred to in Article 47, plans to be submitted to the Members of the United Nations for the establishment of a system for the regulation of armaments.

Voting

Article 27

1. Each member of the Security Council shall have one vote.
2. Decisions of the Security Council on procedural matters shall be made by an affirmative vote of nine members.
3. Decisions of the Security Council on all other matters shall be made by an affirmative vote of nine members including the concurring votes of the permanent members; provided that, in decisions under Chapter VI, and under paragraph 3 of Article 52, a party to a dispute shall abstain from voting.

Procedure

Article 28

1. The Security Council shall be so organized as to be able to function continuously. Each member of the Security Council shall for this purpose be represented at all times at the seat of the Organization.
2. The Security Council shall hold periodic meetings at which each of its members may, if it so desires, be represented by a member of the government or by some other specially designated representative.
3. The Security Council may hold meetings at such places other than the seat of the Organization as in its judgment will best facilitate its work.

Article 29

The Security Council may establish such subsidiary organs as it deems necessary for the performance of its functions.

Article 30

The Security Council shall adopt its own rules of procedure, including the method of selecting its President.

Article 31

Any Member of the United Nations which is not a member of the

Security Council may participate, without vote, in the discussion of any question brought before the Security Council whenever the latter considers that the interests of that Member are specially affected.

Article 32

Any Member of the United Nations which is not a member of the Security Council or any state which is not a Member of the United Nations, if it is a party to a dispute under consideration by the Security Council, shall be invited to participate, without vote, in the discussion relating to the dispute. The Security Council shall lay down such conditions as it deems just for the participation of a state which is not a Member of the United Nations.

Chapter VI   Pacific Settlement of Disputes

Article 33

1. The parties to any dispute, the continuance of which is likely to endanger the maintenance of international peace and security, shall, first of all, seek a solution by negotiation, enquiry, mediation, conciliation, arbitration, judicial settlement, resort to regional agencies or arrangements, or other peaceful means of their own choice.
2. The Security Council shall, when it deems necessary, call upon the parties to settle their dispute by such means.

Article 34

The Security Council may investigate any dispute, or any situation which might lead to international friction or give rise to a dispute, in order to determine whether the continuance of the dispute or situation is likely to endanger the maintenance of international peace and security.

Article 35

1. Any Member of the United Nations may bring any dispute, or any

situation of the nature referred to in Article 34, to the attention
of the Security Council or of the General Assembly.

2. A state which is not a Member of the United Nations may bring to
the attention of the Security Council or of the General Assembly
any dispute to which it is a party if it accepts in advance, for the
purposes of the dispute, the obligations of pacific settlement provided in the present Charter.

3. The proceedings of the General Assembly in respect of matters
brought to its attention under this Article will be subject to the
provisions of Articles 11 and 12.

Article 36

1. The Security Council may, at any stage of a dispute of the nature
referred to in Article 33 or of a situation of like nature, recommend appropriate procedures or methods of adjustment.

2. The Security Council should take into consideration any procedures for the settlement of the dispute which have already been
adopted by the parties.

3. In making recommendations under this Article the Security Council should also take into consideration that legal disputes should
as a general rule be referred by the parties to the International
Court of Justice in accordance with the provisions of the Statute
of the Court.

Article 37

1. Should the parties to a dispute of the nature referred to in Article
33 fail to settle it by the means indicated in that Article, they
shall refer it to the Security Council.

2. If the Security Council deems that the continuance of the dispute
is in fact likely to endanger the maintenance of international peace
and security, it shall decide whether to take action under Article
36 or to recommend such terms of settlement as it may consider
appropriate.

Article 38

Without prejudice to the provisions of Articles 33 to 37, the Security Council may, if all the parties to any dispute so request, make recommendations to the parties with a view to a pacific settlement of the dispute.

Chapter VII   Action with Respect to Threats to the Peace, Breaches of the Peace, and Acts of Aggression

Article 39

The Security Council shall determine the existence of any threat to the peace, breach of the peace, or act of aggression and shall make recommendations, or decide what measures shall be taken in accordance with Articles 41 and 42, to maintain or restore international peace and security.

Article 40

In order to prevent an aggravation of the situation, the Security Council may, before making the recommendations or deciding upon the measures provided for in Article 39, call upon the parties concerned to comply with such provisional measures as it deems necessary or desirable. Such provisional measures shall be without prejudice to the rights, claims, or position of the parties concerned. The Security Council shall duly take account of failure to comply with such provisional measures.

Article 41

The Security Council may decide what measures not involving the use of armed force are to be employed to give effect to its decisions, and it may call upon the Members of the United Nations to apply such measures. These may include complete or partial interruption of economic relations and of rail, sea, air, postal, telegraphic, radio, and other means of communication, and the severance of diplomatic relations.

Article 42

Should the Security Council consider that measures provided for in Article 41 would be inadequate or have proved to be inadequate, it may take such action by air, sea, or land forces as may be necessary to maintain or restore international peace and security. Such action may include demonstrations, blockade, and other operations by air, sea, or land forces of Members of the United Nations.

Article 43

1. All Members of the United Nations, in order to contribute to the maintenance of international peace and security, undertake to make available to the Security Council, on its call and in accordance with a special agreement or agreements, armed forces, assistance, and facilities, including rights of passage, necessary for the purpose of maintaining international peace and security.
2. Such agreement or agreements shall govern the numbers and types of forces, their degree of readiness and general location, and the nature of the facilities and assistance to be provided.
3. The agreement or agreements shall be negotiated as soon as possible on the initiative of the Security Council. They shall be concluded between the Security Council and Members or between the Security Council and groups of Members and shall be subject to ratification by the signatory states in accordance with their respective constitutional processes.

Article 44

When the Security Council has decided to use force it shall, before calling upon a Member not represented on it to provide armed forces in fulfillment of the obligations assumed under Article 43, invite that Member, if the Member so desires, to participate in the decisions of the Security Council concerning the employment of contingents of that Member's armed forces.

Article 45

In order to enable the United Nations to take urgent military measures, Members shall hold immediately available national air-force contingents for combined international enforcement action. The strength and degree of readiness of these contingents and plans for their combined action shall be determined within the limits laid down in the special agreement or agreements referred to in Article 43, by the Security Council with the assistance of the Military Staff Committee.

Article 46
Plans for the application of armed force shall be made by the Security Council with the assistance of the Military Staff Committee.

Article 47
1. There shall be established a Military Staff Committee to advise and assist the Security Council on all questions relating to the Security Council's military requirements for the maintenance of international peace and security, the employment and command of forces placed at its disposal, the regulation of armaments, and possible disarmament.
2. The Military Staff Committee shall consist of the Chiefs of Staff of the permanent members of the Security Council or their representatives. Any Member of the United Nations not permanently represented on the Committee shall be invited by the Committee to be associated with it when the efficient discharge of the Committee's responsibilities requires the participation of that Member in its work.
3. The Military Staff Committee shall be responsible under the Security Council for the strategic direction of any armed forces placed at the disposal of the Security Council. Questions relating to the command of such forces shall be worked out subsequently.
4. The Military Staff Committee, with the authorization of the Security Council and after consultation with appropriate regional agencies, may establish regional subcommittees.

Article 48

1. The action required to carry out the decisions of the Security Council for the maintenance of international peace and security shall be taken by all the Members of the United Nations or by some of them, as the Security Council may determine.
2. Such decisions shall be carried out by the Members of the United Nations directly and through their action in the appropriate international agencies of which they are members.

Article 49

The Members of the United Nations shall join in affording mutual assistance in carrying out the measures decided upon by the Security Council.

Article 50

If preventive or enforcement measures against any state are taken by the Security Council, any other state, whether a Member of the United Nations or not, which finds itself confronted with special economic problems arising from the carrying out of those measures shall have the right to consult the Security Council with regard to a solution of those problems.

Article 51

Nothing in the present Charter shall impair the inherent right of individual or collective self-defence if an armed attack occurs against a Member of the United Nations, until the Security Council has taken measures necessary to maintain international peace and security. Measures taken by Members in the exercise of this right of self-defence shall be immediately reported to the Security Council and shall not in any way affect the authority and responsibility of the Security Council under the present Charter to take at any time such action as it deems necessary in order to maintain or restore international peace and security.

Chapter VIII   Regional Arrangements

Article 52

1. Nothing in the present Charter precludes the existence of regional arrangements or agencies for dealing with such matters relating to the maintenance of international peace and security as are appropriate for regional action provided that such arrangements or agencies and their activities are consistent with the Purposes and Principles of the United Nations.

2. The Members of the United Nations entering into such arrangements or constituting such agencies shall make every effort to achieve pacific settlement of local disputes through such regional arrangements or by such regional agencies before referring them to the Security Council.

3. The Security Council shall encourage the development of pacific settlement of local disputes through such regional arrangements or by such regional agencies either on the initiative of the states concerned or by reference from the Security Council.

4. This Article in no way impairs the application of Articles 34 and 35.

Article 53

1. The Security Council shall, where appropriate, utilize such regional arrangements or agencies for enforcement action under its authority. But no enforcement action shall be taken under regional arrangements or by regional agencies without the authorization of the Security Council, with the exception of measures against any enemy state, as defined in paragraph 2 of this Article, provided for pursuant to Article 107 or in regional arrangements directed against renewal of aggressive policy on the part of any such state, until such time as the Organization may, on request of the Governments concerned, be charged with the responsibility for preventing further aggression by such a state.

2. The term enemy state as used in paragraph 1 of this Article applies to any state which during the Second World War has been

an enemy of any signatory of the present Charter.

Article 54

The Security Council shall at all times be kept fully informed of activities undertaken or in contemplation under regional arrangements or by regional agencies for the maintenance of international peace and security.

Chapter IX International Economic and Social Cooperation

Article 55

With a view to the creation of conditions of stability and well-being which are necessary for peaceful and friendly relations among nations based on respect for the principle of equal rights and self-determination of peoples, the United Nations shall promote:

a. higher standards of living, full employment, and conditions of economic and social progress and development;

b. solutions of international economic, social, health, and related problems; and international cultural and educational cooperation; and

c. universal respect for, and observance of, human rights and fundamental freedoms for all without distinction as to race, sex, language, or religion.

Article 56

All Members pledge themselves to take joint and separate action in cooperation with the Organization for the achievement of the purposes set forth in Article 55.

Article 57

1. The various specialized agencies, established by intergovernmental agreement and having wide international responsibilities, as defined in their basic instruments, in economic, social, cultural, educational, health, and related fields, shall be brought into rela-

tionship with the United Nations in accordance with the provisions of Article 63.

2. Such agencies thus brought into relationship with the United Nations are hereinafter referred to as specialized agencies.

Article 58

The Organization shall make recommendations for the coordination of the policies and activities of the specialized agencies.

Article 59

The Organization shall, where appropriate, initiate negotiations among the states concerned for the creation of any new specialized agencies required for the accomplishment of the purposes set forth in Article 55.

Article 60

Responsibility for the discharge of the functions of the Organization set forth in this Chapter shall be vested in the General Assembly and, under the authority of the General Assembly, in the Economic and Social Council, which shall have for this purpose the powers set forth in Chapter X.

Chapter X   The Economic And Social Council
Composition
Article 61

1. The Economic and Social Council shall consist of fifty-four Members of the United Nations elected by the General Assembly.

2. Subject to the provisions of paragraph 3, eighteen members of the Economic and Social Council shall be elected each year for a term of three years. A retiring member shall be eligible for immediate re-election.

3. At the first election after the increase in the membership of the Economic and Social Council from twenty-seven to fifty-four members, in addition to the members elected in place of the nine mem-

bers whose term of office expires at the end of that year, twenty-seven additional members shall be elected. Of these twenty-seven additional members, the term of office of nine members so elected shall expire at the end of one year, and of nine other members at the end of two years, in accordance with arrangements made by the General Assembly.

4. Each member of the Economic and Social Council shall have one representative.

Functions and Powers
Article 62

1. The Economic and Social Council may make or initiate studies and reports with respect to international economic, social, cultural, educational, health, and related matters and may make recommendations with respect to any such matters to the General Assembly to the Members of the United Nations, and to the specialized agencies concerned.

2. It may make recommendations for the purpose of promoting respect for, and observance of, human rights and fundamental freedoms for all.

3. It may prepare draft conventions for submission to the General Assembly, with respect to matters falling within its competence.

4. It may call, in accordance with the rules prescribed by the United Nations, international conferences on matters falling within its competence.

Article 63

1. The Economic and Social Council may enter into agreements with any of the agencies referred to in Article 57, defining the terms on which the agency concerned shall be brought into relationship with the United Nations. Such agreements shall be subject to approval by the General Assembly.

2. It may coordinate the activities of the specialized agencies through consultation with and recommendations to such agencies and

through recommendations to the General Assembly and to the Members of the United Nations.

Article 64

1. The Economic and Social Council may take appropriate steps to obtain regular reports from the specialized agencies. It may make arrangements with the Members of the United Nations and with the specialized agencies to obtain reports on the steps taken to give effect to its own recommendations and to recommendations on matters falling within its competence made by the General Assembly.
2. It may communicate its observations on these reports to the General Assembly.

Article 65

The Economic and Social Council may furnish information to the Security Council and shall assist the Security Council upon its request.

Article 66

1. The Economic and Social Council shall perform such functions as fall within its competence in connection with the carrying out of the recommendations of the General Assembly.
2. It may, with the approval of the General Assembly, perform services at the request of Members of the United Nations and at the request of specialized agencies.
3. It shall perform such other functions as are specified elsewhere in the present Charter or as may be assigned to it by the General Assembly.

Voting
Article 67

1. Each member of the Economic and Social Council shall have one vote.

2. Decisions of the Economic and Social Council shall be made by a majority of the members present and voting.

Procedure
Article 68
The Economic and Social Council shall set up commissions in economic and social fields and for the promotion of human rights, and such other commissions as may be required for the performance of its functions.

Article 69
The Economic and Social Council shall invite any Member of the United Nations to participate, without vote, in its deliberations on any matter of particular concern to that Member.

Article 70
The Economic and Social Council may make arrangements for representatives of the specialized agencies to participate, without vote, in its deliberations and in those of the commissions established by it, and for its representatives to participate in the deliberations of the specialized agencies.

Article 71
The Economic and Social Council may make suitable arrangements for consultation with nongovernmental organizations which are concerned with matters within its competence. Such arrangements may be made with international organizations and, where appropriate, with national organizations after consultation with the Member of the United Nations concerned.

Article 72
1. The Economic and Social Council shall adopt its own rules of procedure, including the method of selecting its President.

2. The Economic and Social Council shall meet as required in accordance with its rules, which shall include provision for the convening of meetings on the request of a majority of its members.

Chapter XI　Declaration Regarding Non-Self-Governing Territories

Article 73

Members of the United Nations which have or assume responsibilities for the administration of territories whose peoples have not yet attained a full measure of self-government recognize the principle that the interests of the inhabitants of these territories are paramount, and accept as a sacred trust the obligation to promote to the utmost, within the system of international peace and security established by the present Charter, the well-being of the inhabitants of these territories, and, to this end:

a. to ensure, with due respect for the culture of the peoples concerned, their political, economic, social, and educational advancement, their just treatment, and their protection against abuses;

b. to develop self-government, to take due account of the political aspirations of the peoples, and to assist them in the progressive development of their free political institutions, according to the particular circumstances of each territory and its peoples and their varying stages of advancement;

c. to further international peace and security;

d. to promote constructive measures of development, to encourage research, and to cooperate with one another and, when and where appropriate, with specialized international bodies with a view to the practical achievement of the social, economic, and scientific purposes set forth in this Article; and

e. to transmit regularly to the Secretary-General for information purposes, subject to such limitation as security and constitutional considerations may require, statistical and other information of a technical nature relating to economic, social, and educational conditions in the territories for which they are respectively responsible other than those territories to which Chapters XII and XIII apply.

Article 74

Members of the United Nations also agree that their policy in respect of the territories to which this Chapter applies, no less than in respect of their metropolitan areas, must be based on the general principle of good-neighbourliness, due account being taken of the interests and well-being of the rest of the world, in social, economic, and commercial matters.

Chapter XII International Trusteeship System

Article 75

The United Nations shall establish under its authority an international trusteeship system for the administration and supervision of such territories as may be placed thereunder by subsequent individual agreements. These territories are hereinafter referred to as trust territories.

Article 76

The basic objectives of the trusteeship system, in accordance with the Purposes of the United Nations laid down in Article 1 of the present Charter, shall be:

a. to further international peace and security;

b. to promote the political, economic, social, and educational advancement of the inhabitants of the trust territories, and their progressive development towards self-government or independence as may be appropriate to the particular circumstances of each territory and its peoples and the freely expressed wishes of the peoples concerned, and as may be provided by the terms of each trusteeship agreement;

c. to encourage respect for human rights and for fundamental freedoms for all without distinction as to race, sex, language, or religion, and to encourage recognition of the interdependence of the peoples of the world; and

d. to ensure equal treatment in social, economic, and commercial matters for all Members of the United Nations and their nationals, and also equal treatment for the latter in the administration of justice, without prejudice to the attainment of the foregoing objectives and subject to the provisions of Article 80.

Article 77

1. The trusteeship system shall apply to such territories in the following categories as may be placed thereunder by means of trusteeship agreements:
   a. territories now held under mandate;
   b. territories which may be detached from enemy states as a result of the Second World War; and
   c. territories voluntarily placed under the system by states responsible for their administration.
2. It will be a matter for subsequent agreement as to which territories in the foregoing categories will be brought under the trusteeship system and upon what terms.

Article 78

The trusteeship system shall not apply to territories which have become Members of the United Nations, relationship among which shall be based on respect for the principle of sovereign equality.

Article 79

The terms of trusteeship for each territory to be placed under the trusteeship system, including any alteration or amendment, shall be agreed upon by the states directly concerned, including the mandatory power in the case of territories held under mandate by a Member of the United Nations, and shall be approved as provided for in Articles 83 and 85.

Article 80

1. Except as may be agreed upon in individual trusteeship agree-

ments, made under Articles 77, 79, and 81, placing each territory under the trusteeship system, and until such agreements have been concluded, nothing in this Chapter shall be construed in or of itself to alter in any manner the rights whatsoever of any states or any peoples or the terms of existing international instruments to which Members of the United Nations may respectively be parties.

2. Paragraph 1 of this Article shall not be interpreted as giving grounds for delay or postponement of the negotiation and conclusion of agreements for placing mandated and other territories under the trusteeship system as provided for in Article 77.

Article 81

The trusteeship agreement shall in each case include the terms under which the trust territory will be administered and designate the authority which will exercise the administration of the trust territory. Such authority, hereinafter called the administering authority, may be one or more states or the Organization itself.

Article 82

There may be designated, in any trusteeship agreement, a strategic area or areas which may include part or all of the trust territory to which the agreement applies, without prejudice to any special agreement or agreements made under Article 43.

Article 83

1. All functions of the United Nations relating to strategic areas, including the approval of the terms of the trusteeship agreements and of their alteration or amendment shall be exercised by the Security Council.

2. The basic objectives set forth in Article 76 shall be applicable to the people of each strategic area.

3. The Security Council shall, subject to the provisions of the trusteeship agreements and without prejudice to security consider-

ations, avail itself of the assistance of the Trusteeship Council to perform those functions of the United Nations under the trusteeship system relating to political, economic, social, and educational matters in the strategic areas.

Article 84

It shall be the duty of the administering authority to ensure that the trust territory shall play its part in the maintenance of international peace and security. To this end the administering authority may make use of volunteer forces, facilities, and assistance from the trust territory in carrying out the obligations towards the Security Council undertaken in this regard by the administering authority, as well as for local defence and the maintenance of law and order within the trust territory.

Article 85

1. The functions of the United Nations with regard to trusteeship agreements for all areas not designated as strategic, including the approval of the terms of the trusteeship agreements and of their alteration or amendment, shall be exercised by the General Assembly.
2. The Trusteeship Council, operating under the authority of the General Assembly shall assist the General Assembly in carrying out these functions.

Chapter XIII   The Trusteeship Council
Composition
Article 86

1. The Trusteeship Council shall consist of the following Members of the United Nations:
   a. those Members administering trust territories;
   b. such of those Members mentioned by name in Article 23 as are not administering trust territories; and
   c. as many other Members elected for three-year terms by the

General Assembly as may be necessary to ensure that the total number of members of the Trusteeship Council is equally divided between those Members of the United Nations which administer trust territories and those which do not.

2. Each member of the Trusteeship Council shall designate one specially qualified person to represent it therein.

Functions and Powers
Article 87
The General Assembly and, under its authority, the Trusteeship Council, in carrying out their functions, may:

a. consider reports submitted by the administering authority;

b. accept petitions and examine them in consultation with the administering authority;

c. provide for periodic visits to the respective trust territories at times agreed upon with the administering authority; and

d. take these and other actions in conformity with the terms of the trusteeship agreements.

Article 88
The Trusteeship Council shall formulate a questionnaire on the political, economic, social, and educational advancement of the inhabitants of each trust territory, and the administering authority for each trust territory within the competence of the General Assembly shall make an annual report to the General Assembly upon the basis of such questionnaire.

Voting
Article 89
1. Each member of the Trusteeship Council shall have one vote.

2. Decisions of the Trusteeship Council shall be made by a majority of the members present and voting.

Procedure
Article 90
1. The Trusteeship Council shall adopt its own rules of procedure,

including the method of selecting its President.

2. The Trusteeship Council shall meet as required in accordance with its rules, which shall include provision for the convening of meetings on the request of a majority of its members.

Article 91

The Trusteeship Council shall, when appropriate, avail itself of the assistance of the Economic and Social Council and of the specialized agencies in regard to matters with which they are respectively concerned.

Chapter XIV   The International Court of Justice
Article 92

The International Court of Justice shall be the principal judicial organ of the United Nations. It shall function in accordance with the annexed Statute, which is based upon the Statute of the Permanent Court of International Justice and forms an integral part of the present Charter.

Article 93

1. All Members of the United Nations are ipso facto parties to the Statute of the International Court of Justice.

2. A state which is not a Member of the United Nations may become a party to the Statute of the International Court of Justice on conditions to be determined in each case by the General Assembly upon the recommendation of the Security Council.

Article 94

1. Each Member of the United Nations undertakes to comply with the decision of the International Court of Justice in any case to which it is a party.

2. If any party to a case fails to perform the obligations incumbent upon it under a judgment rendered by the Court, the other party may have recourse to the Security Council, which may, if it deems

necessary, make recommendations or decide upon measures to be taken to give effect to the judgment.

Article 95

Nothing in the present Charter shall prevent Members of the United Nations from entrusting the solution of their differences to other tribunals by virtue of agreements already in existence or which may be concluded in the future.

Article 96

1. The General Assembly or the Security Council may request the International Court of Justice to give an advisory opinion on any legal question.
2. Other organs of the United Nations and specialized agencies, which may at any time be so authorized by the General Assembly, may also request advisory opinions of the Court on legal questions arising within the scope of their activities.

Chapter XV   The Secretariat

Article 97

The Secretariat shall comprise a Secretary-General and such staff as the Organization may require. The Secretary-General shall be appointed by the General Assembly upon the recommendation of the Security Council. He shall be the chief administrative officer of the Organization.

Article 98

The Secretary-General shall act in that capacity in all meetings of the General Assembly, of the Security Council, of the Economic and Social Council, and of the Trusteeship Council, and shall perform such other functions as are entrusted to him by these organs. The Secretary-General shall make an annual report to the General Assembly on the work of the Organization.

Article 99

The Secretary-General may bring to the attention of the Security Council any matter which in his opinion may threaten the maintenance of international peace and security.

Article 100

1. In the performance of their duties the Secretary-General and the staff shall not seek or receive instructions from any government or from any other authority external to the Organization. They shall refrain from any action which might reflect on their position as international officials responsible only to the Organization.
2. Each Member of the United Nations undertakes to respect the exclusively international character of the responsibilities of the Secretary-General and the staff and not to seek to influence them in the discharge of their responsibilities.

Article 101

1. The staff shall be appointed by the Secretary-General under regulations established by the General Assembly.
2. Appropriate staffs shall be permanently assigned to the Economic and Social Council, the Trusteeship Council, and, as required, to other organs of the United Nations. These staffs shall form a part of the Secretariat.
3. The paramount consideration in the employment of the staff and in the determination of the conditions of service shall be the necessity of securing the highest standards of efficiency, competence, and integrity. Due regard shall be paid to the importance of recruiting the staff on as wide a geographical basis as possible.

Chapter XVI   Miscellaneous Provisions

Article 102

1. Every treaty and every international agreement entered into by any Member of the United Nations after the present Charter

comes into force shall as soon as possible be registered with the Secretariat and published by it.

2. No party to any such treaty or international agreement which has not been registered in accordance with the provisions of paragraph 1 of this Article may invoke that treaty or agreement before any organ of the United Nations.

Article 103

In the event of a conflict between the obligations of the Members of the United Nations under the present Charter and their obligations under any other international agreement, their obligations under the present Charter shall prevail.

Article 104

The Organization shall enjoy in the territory of each of its Members such legal capacity as may be necessary for the exercise of its functions and the fulfillment of its purposes.

Article 105

1. The Organization shall enjoy in the territory of each of its Members such privileges and immunities as are necessary for the fulfillment of its purposes.

2. Representatives of the Members of the United Nations and officials of the Organization shall similarly enjoy such privileges and immunities as are necessary for the independent exercise of their functions in connection with the Organization.

3. The General Assembly may make recommendations with a view to determining the details of the application of paragraphs 1 and 2 of this Article or may propose conventions to the Members of the United Nations for this purpose.

Chapter XVII   Transitional Security Arrangements
Article 106

Pending the coming into force of such special agreements referred to in Article 43 as in the opinion of the Security Council enable it to begin the exercise of its responsibilities under Article 42, the parties to the Four-Nation Declaration, signed at Moscow, 30 October 1943, and France, shall, in accordance with the provisions of paragraph 5 of that Declaration, consult with one another and as occasion requires with other Members of the United Nations with a view to such joint action on behalf of the Organization as may be necessary for the purpose of maintaining international peace and security.

Article 107
Nothing in the present Charter shall invalidate or preclude action, in relation to any state which during the Second World War has been an enemy of any signatory to the present Charter, taken or authorized as a result of that war by the Governments having responsibility for such action.

Chapter XVIII   Amendments
Article 108
Amendments to the present Charter shall come into force for all Members of the United Nations when they have been adopted by a vote of two thirds of the members of the General Assembly and ratified in accordance with their respective constitutional processes by two thirds of the Members of the United Nations, including all the permanent members of the Security Council.

Article 109
1. A General Conference of the Members of the United Nations for the purpose of reviewing the present Charter may be held at a date and place to be fixed by a two-thirds vote of the members of the General Assembly and by a vote of any nine members of the Security Council. Each Member of the United Nations shall have one vote in the conference.
2. Any alteration of the present Charter recommended by a two-

thirds vote of the conference shall take effect when ratified in accordance with their respective constitutional processes by two thirds of the Members of the United Nations including all the permanent members of the Security Council.

3. If such a conference has not been held before the tenth annual session of the General Assembly following the coming into force of the present Charter, the proposal to call such a conference shall be placed on the agenda of that session of the General Assembly, and the conference shall be held if so decided by a majority vote of the members of the General Assembly and by a vote of any seven members of the Security Council.

Chapter XIX   Ratification and Signature

Article 110

1. The present Charter shall be ratified by the signatory states in accordance with their respective constitutional processes.
2. The ratifications shall be deposited with the Government of the United States of America, which shall notify all the signatory states of each deposit as well as the Secretary-General of the Organization when he has been appointed.
3. The present Charter shall come into force upon the deposit of ratifications by the Republic of China, France, the Union of Soviet Socialist Republics, the United Kingdom of Great Britain and Northern Ireland, and the United States of America, and by a majority of the other signatory states. A protocol of the ratifications deposited shall thereupon be drawn up by the Government of the United States of America which shall communicate copies thereof to all the signatory states.
4. The states signatory to the present Charter which ratify it after it has come into force will become original Members of the United Nations on the date of the deposit of their respective ratifications.

Article 111

The present Charter, of which the Chinese, French, Russian, English, and Spanish texts are equally authentic, shall remain deposited in the archives of the Government of the United States of America. Duly certified copies thereof shall be transmitted by that Government to the Governments of the other signatory states.

IN FAITH WHEREOF the representatives of the Governments of the United Nations have signed the present Charter.

DONE at the city of San Francisco the twenty-sixth day of June, one thousand nine hundred and forty-five.

■ ■ ■ ■ ■

STATUTE OF
THE INTERNATIONAL COURT OF JUSTICE

Article 1

The International Court of Justice established by the Charter of the United Nations as the principal judicial organ of the United Nations shall be constituted and shall function in accordance with the provisions of the present Statute.

Chapter I   Organization Of The Court
Article 2

The Court shall be composed of a body of independent judges, elected regardless of their nationality from among persons of high moral character, who possess the qualifications required in their respective countries for appointment to the highest judicial offices, or are jurisconsults of recognized competence in international law.

Article 3

1. The Court shall consist of fifteen members, no two of whom may be nationals of the same state.
2. A person who for the purposes of membership in the Court could be regarded as a national of more than one state shall be deemed to be a national of the one in which he ordinarily exercises civil and political rights.

Article 4

1. The members of the Court shall be elected by the General Assembly and by the Security Council from a list of persons nominated by the national groups in the Permanent Court of Arbitration, in accordance with the following provisions.

2. In the case of Members of the United Nations not represented in the Permanent Court of Arbitration, candidates shall be nominated by national groups appointed for this purpose by their governments under the same conditions as those prescribed for members of the Permanent Court of Arbitration by Article 44 of the Convention of The Hague of 1907 for the pacific settlement of international disputes.

3. The conditions under which a state which is a party to the present Statute but is not a Member of the United Nations may participate in electing the members of the Court shall, in the absence of a special agreement, be laid down by the General Assembly upon recommendation of the Security Council.

Article 5

1. At least three months before the date of the election, the Secretary-General of the United Nations shall address a written request to the members of the Permanent Court of Arbitration belonging to the states which are parties to the present Statute, and to the members of the national groups appointed under Article 4, paragraph 2, inviting them to undertake, within a given time, by national groups, the nomination of persons in a position to accept the duties of a member of the Court.

2. No group may nominate more than four persons, not more than two of whom shall be of their own nationality. In no case may the number of candidates nominated by a group be more than double the number of seats to be filled.

Article 6

Before making these nominations, each national group is recommended to consult its highest court of justice, its legal faculties and schools of law, and its national academies and national sections of international academies devoted to the study of law.

Article 7

1. The Secretary-General shall prepare a list in alphabetical order of all the persons thus nominated. Save as provided in Article 12, paragraph 2, these shall be the only persons eligible.
2. The Secretary-General shall submit this list to the General Assembly and to the Security Council.

Article 8

The General Assembly and the Security Council shall proceed independently of one another to elect the members of the Court.

Article 9

At every election, the electors shall bear in mind not only that the persons to be elected should individually possess the qualifications required, but also that in the body as a whole the representation of the main forms of civilization and of the principal legal systems of the world should be assured.

Article 10

1. Those candidates who obtain an absolute majority of votes in the General Assembly and in the Security Council shall be considered as elected.
2. Any vote of the Security Council, whether for the election of judges or for the appointment of members of the conference envisaged in Article 12, shall be taken without any distinction between permanent and non-permanent members of the Security Council.
3. In the event of more than one national of the same state obtaining an absolute majority of the votes both of the General Assembly and of the Security Council, the eldest of these only shall be considered as elected.

Article 11

If, after the first meeting held for the purpose of the election, one or more seats remain to be filled, a second and, if necessary, a third meeting shall take place.

Article 12

1. If, after the third meeting, one or more seats still remain unfilled, a joint conference consisting of six members, three appointed by the General Assembly and three by the Security Council, may be formed at any time at the request of either the General Assembly or the Security Council, for the purpose of choosing by the vote of an absolute majority one name for each seat still vacant, to submit to the General Assembly and the Security Council for their respective acceptance.

2. If the joint conference is unanimously agreed upon any person who fulfills the required conditions, he may be included in its list, even though he was not included in the list of nominations referred to in Article 7.

3. If the joint conference is satisfied that it will not be successful in procuring an election, those members of the Court who have already been elected shall, within a period to be fixed by the Security Council, proceed to fill the vacant seats by selection from among those candidates who have obtained votes either in the General Assembly or in the Security Council.

4. In the event of an equality of votes among the judges, the eldest judge shall have a casting vote.

Article 13

1. The members of the Court shall be elected for nine years and may be re-elected; provided, however, that of the judges elected at the first election, the terms of five judges shall expire at the end of three years and the terms of five more judges shall expire at the end of six years.

2. The judges whose terms are to expire at the end of the above-

mentioned initial periods of three and six years shall be chosen by lot to be drawn by the Secretary-General immediately after the first election has been completed.

3. The members of the Court shall continue to discharge their duties until their places have been filled. Though replaced, they shall finish any cases which they may have begun.

4. In the case of the resignation of a member of the Court, the resignation shall be addressed to the President of the Court for transmission to the Secretary-General. This last notification makes the place vacant.

Article 14

Vacancies shall be filled by the same method as that laid down for the first election subject to the following provision: the Secretary-General shall, within one month of the occurrence of the vacancy, proceed to issue the invitations provided for in Article 5, and the date of the election shall be fixed by the Security Council.

Article 15

A member of the Court elected to replace a member whose term of office has not expired shall hold office for the remainder of his predecessor's term.

Article 16

1. No member of the Court may exercise any political or administrative function, or engage in any other occupation of a professional nature.

2. Any doubt on this point shall be settled by the decision of the Court.

Article 17

1. No member of the Court may act as agent, counsel, or advocate in any case.

2. No member may participate in the decision of any case in which

he has previously taken part as agent, counsel, or advocate for one of the parties, or as a member of a national or international court, or of a commission of enquiry, or in any other capacity.

3. Any doubt on this point shall be settled by the decision of the Court.

Article 18

1. No member of the Court can be dismissed unless, in the unanimous opinion of the other members, he has ceased to fulfill the required conditions.
2. Formal notification thereof shall be made to the Secretary-General by the Registrar.
3. This notification makes the place vacant.

Article 19

The members of the Court, when engaged on the business of the Court, shall enjoy diplomatic privileges and immunities.

Article 20

Every member of the Court shall, before taking up his duties, make a solemn declaration in open court that he will exercise his powers impartially and conscientiously.

Article 21

1. The Court shall elect its President and Vice-President for three years; they may be re-elected.
2. The Court shall appoint its Registrar and may provide for the appointment of such other officers as may be necessary.

Article 22

1. The seat of the Court shall be established at The Hague. This, however, shall not prevent the Court from sitting and exercising its functions elsewhere whenever the Court considers it desirable.

2. The President and the Registrar shall reside at the seat of the Court.

Article 23

1. The Court shall remain permanently in session, except during the judicial vacations, the dates and duration of which shall be fixed by the Court.
2. Members of the Court are entitled to periodic leave, the dates and duration of which shall be fixed by the Court, having in mind the distance between The Hague and the home of each judge.
3. Members of the Court shall be bound, unless they are on leave or prevented from attending by illness or other serious reasons duly explained to the President, to hold themselves permanently at the disposal of the Court.

Article 24

1. If, for some special reason, a member of the Court considers that he should not take part in the decision of a particular case, he shall so inform the President.
2. If the President considers that for some special reason one of the members of the Court should not sit in a particular case, he shall give him notice accordingly.
3. If in any such case the member Court and the President disagree, the matter shall be settled by the decision of the Court.

Article 25

1. The full Court shall sit except when it is expressly provided otherwise in the present Statute.
2. Subject to the condition that the number of judges available to constitute the Court is not thereby reduced below eleven, the Rules of the Court may provide for allowing one or more judges, according to circumstances and in rotation, to be dispensed from sitting.
3. A quorum of nine judges shall suffice to constitute the Court.

Article 26

1. The Court may from time to time form one or more chambers, composed of three or more judges as the Court may determine, for dealing with particular categories of cases; for example, labour cases and cases relating to transit and communications.
2. The Court may at any time form a chamber for dealing with a particular case. The number of judges to constitute such a chamber shall be determined by the Court with the approval of the parties.
3. Cases shall be heard and determined by the chambers provided for in this article if the parties so request.

Article 27

A judgment given by any of the chambers provided for in Articles 26 and 29 shall be considered as rendered by the Court.

Article 28

The chambers provided for in Articles 26 and 29 may, with the consent of the parties, sit and exercise their functions elsewhere than at The Hague.

Article 29

With a view to the speedy dispatch of business, the Court shall form annually a chamber composed of five judges which, at the request of the parties, may hear and determine cases by summary procedure. In addition, two judges shall be selected for the purpose of replacing judges who find it impossible to sit.

Article 30

1. The Court shall frame rules for carrying out its functions. In particular, it shall lay down rules of procedure.
2. The Rules of the Court may provide for assessors to sit with the Court or with any of its chambers, without the right to vote.

Article 31

1. Judges of the nationality of each of the parties shall retain their right to sit in the case before the Court.
2. If the Court includes upon the Bench a judge of the nationality of one of the parties, any other party may choose a person to sit as judge. Such person shall be chosen preferably from among those persons who have been nominated as candidates as provided in Articles 4 and 5.
3. If the Court includes upon the Bench no judge of the nationality of the parties, each of these parties may proceed to choose a judge as provided in paragraph 2 of this Article.
4. The provisions of this Article shall apply to the case of Articles 26 and 29. In such cases, the President shall request one or, if necessary, two of the members of the Court forming the chamber to give place to the members of the Court of the nationality of the parties concerned, and, failing such, or if they are unable to be present, to the judges specially chosen by the parties.
5. Should there be several parties in the same interest, they shall, for the purpose of the preceding provisions, be reckoned as one party only. Any doubt upon this point shall be settled by the decision of the Court.
6. Judges chosen as laid down in paragraphs 2, 3, and 4 of this Article shall fulfill the conditions required by Articles 2, 17 (paragraph 2), 20, and 24 of the present Statute. They shall take part in the decision on terms of complete equality with their colleagues.

Article 32

1. Each member of the Court shall receive an annual salary.
2. The President shall receive a special annual allowance.
3. The Vice-President shall receive a special allowance for every day on which he acts as President.
4. The judges chosen under Article 31, other than members of the Court, shall receive compensation for each day on which they exercise their functions.

5. These salaries, allowances, and compensation shall be fixed by the General Assembly. They may not be decreased during the term of office.

6. The salary of the Registrar shall be fixed by the General Assembly on the proposal of the Court.

7. Regulations made by the General Assembly shall fix the conditions under which retirement pensions may be given to members of the Court and to the Registrar, and the conditions under which members of the Court and the Registrar shall have their travelling expenses refunded.

8. The above salaries, allowances, and compensation shall be free of all taxation.

Article 33

The expenses of the Court shall be borne by the United Nations in such a manner as shall be decided by the General Assembly.

Chapter II   Competence of the Court

Article 34

1. Only states may be parties in cases before the Court.

2. The Court, subject to and in conformity with its Rules, may request of public international organizations information relevant to cases before it, and shall receive such information presented by such organizations on their own initiative.

3. Whenever the construction of the constituent instrument of a public international organization or of an international convention adopted thereunder is in question in a case before the Court, the Registrar shall so notify the public international organization concerned and shall communicate to it copies of all the written proceedings.

Article 35

1. The Court shall be open to the states parties to the present Statute.

2. The conditions under which the Court shall be open to other states shall, subject to the special provisions contained in treaties in force, be laid down by the Security Council, but in no case shall such conditions place the parties in a position of inequality before the Court.

3. When a state which is not a Member of the United Nations is a party to a case, the Court shall fix the amount which that party is to contribute towards the expenses of the Court. This provision shall not apply if such state is bearing a share of the expenses of the Court.

Article 36

1. The jurisdiction of the Court comprises all cases which the parties refer to it and all matters specially provided for in the Charter of the United Nations or in treaties and conventions in force.

2. The states parties to the present Statute may at any time declare that they recognize as compulsory ipso facto and without special agreement, in relation to any other state accepting the same obligation, the jurisdiction of the Court in all legal disputes concerning:

   a. the interpretation of a treaty;

   b. any question of international law;

   c. the existence of any fact which, if established, would constitute a breach of an international obligation;

   d. the nature or extent of the reparation to be made for the breach of an international obligation.

3. The declarations referred to above may be made unconditionally or on condition of reciprocity on the part of several or certain states, or for a certain time.

4. Such declarations shall be deposited with the Secretary-General of the United Nations, who shall transmit copies thereof to the parties to the Statute and to the Registrar of the Court.

5. Declarations made under Article 36 of the Statute of the Permanent Court of International Justice and which are still in force

shall be deemed, as between the parties to the present Statute, to be acceptances of the compulsory jurisdiction of the International Court of Justice for the period which they still have to run and in accordance with their terms.

6. In the event of a dispute as to whether the Court has jurisdiction, the matter shall be settled by the decision of the Court.

Article 37

Whenever a treaty or convention in force provides for reference of a matter to a tribunal to have been instituted by the League of Nations, or to the Permanent Court of International Justice, the matter shall, as between the parties to the present Statute, be referred to the International Court of Justice.

Article 38

1. The Court, whose function is to decide in accordance with international law such disputes as are submitted to it, shall apply:
   a. international conventions, whether general or particular, establishing rules expressly recognized by the contesting states;
   b. international custom, as evidence of a general practice accepted as law;
   c. the general principles of law recognized by civilized nations;
   d. subject to the provisions of Article 59, judicial decisions and the teachings of the most highly qualified publicists of the various nations, as subsidiary means for the determination of rules of law.
2. This provision shall not prejudice the power of the Court to decide a case *ex aequo et bono,* if the parties agree thereto.

Chapter III   Procedure

Article 39

1. The official languages of the Court shall be French and English. If the parties agree that the case shall be conducted in French, the judgment shall be delivered in French. If the parties agree

that the case shall be conducted in English, the judgment shall be delivered in English.

2. In the absence of an agreement as to which language shall be employed, each party may, in the pleadings, use the language which it prefers; the decision of the Court shall be given in French and English. In this case the Court shall at the same time determine which of the two texts shall be considered as authoritative.

3. The Court shall, at the request of any party, authorize a language other than French or English to be used by that party.

Article 40

1. Cases are brought before the Court, as the case may be, either by the notification of the special agreement or by a written application addressed to the Registrar. In either case the subject of the dispute and the parties shall be indicated.

2. The Registrar shall forthwith communicate the application to all concerned.

3. He shall also notify the Members of the United Nations through the Secretary-General, and also any other states entitled to appear before the Court.

Article 41

1. The Court shall have the power to indicate, if it considers that circumstances so require, any provisional measures which ought to be taken to preserve the respective rights of either party.

2. Pending the final decision, notice of the measures suggested shall forthwith be given to the parties and to the Security Council

Article 42

1. The parties shall be represented by agents.

2. They may have the assistance of counsel or advocates before the Court.

3. The agents, counsel, and advocates of parties before the Court shall enjoy the privileges and immunities necessary to the independent exercise of their duties.

Article 43

1. The procedure shall consist of two parts: written and oral.
2. The written proceedings shall consist of the communication to the Court and to the parties of memorials, counter-memorials and, if necessary, replies; also all papers and documents in support.
3. These communications shall be made through the Registrar, in the order and within the time fixed by the Court.
4. A certified copy of every document produced by one party shall be communicated to the other party.
5. The oral proceedings shall consist of the hearing by the Court of witnesses, experts, agents, counsel, and advocates.

Article 44

1. For the service of all notices upon persons other than the agents, counsel, and advocates, the Court shall apply direct to the government of the state upon whose territory the notice has to be served.
2. The same provision shall apply whenever steps are to be taken to procure evidence on the spot.

Article 45

The hearing shall be under the control of the President or, if he is unable to preside, of the Vice-President; if neither is able to preside, the senior judge present shall preside.

Article 46

The hearing in Court shall be public, unless the Court shall decide otherwise, or unless the parties demand that the public be not admitted.

Article 47

1. Minutes shall be made at each hearing and signed by the Registrar and the President.

2. These minutes alone shall be authentic.

Article 48
The Court shall make orders for the conduct of the case, shall decide the form and time in which each party must conclude its arguments, and make all arrangements connected with the taking of evidence.

Article 49
The Court may, even before the hearing begins, call upon the agents to produce any document or to supply any explanations. Formal note shall be taken of any refusal.

Article 50
The Court may, at any time, entrust any individual, body, bureau, commission, or other organization that it may select, with the task of carrying out an enquiry or giving an expert opinion.

Article 51
During the hearing any relevant questions are to be put to the witnesses and experts under the conditions laid down by the Court in the rules of procedure referred to in Article 30.

Article 52
After the Court has received the proofs and evidence within the time specified for the purpose, it may refuse to accept any further oral or written evidence that one party may desire to present unless the other side consents.

Article 53
1. Whenever one of the parties does not appear before the Court, or fails to defend its case, the other party may call upon the Court to decide in favour of its claim.
2. The Court must, before doing so, satisfy itself, not only that it has

jurisdiction in accordance with Articles 36 and 37, but also that the claim is well founded in fact and law.

Article 54

1. When, subject to the control of the Court, the agents, counsel, and advocates have completed their presentation of the case, the President shall declare the hearing closed.
2. The Court shall withdraw to consider the judgment.
3. The deliberations of the Court shall take place in private and remain secret.

Article 55

1. All questions shall be decided by a majority of the judges present.
2. In the event of an equality of votes, the President or the judge who acts in his place shall have a casting vote.

Article 56

1. The judgment shall state the reasons on which it is based.
2. It shall contain the names of the judges who have taken part in the decision.

Article 57

If the judgment does not represent in whole or in part the unanimous opinion of the judges, any judge shall be entitled to deliver a separate opinion.

Article 58

The judgment shall be signed by the President and by the Registrar. It shall be read in open court, due notice having been given to the agents.

Article 59

The decision of the Court has no binding force except between the parties and in respect of that particular case.

Article 60

The judgment is final and without appeal. In the event of dispute as to the meaning or scope of the judgment, the Court shall construe it upon the request of any party.

Article 61

1. An application for revision of a judgment may be made only when it is based upon the discovery of some fact of such a nature as to be a decisive factor, which fact was, when the judgment was given, unknown to the Court and also to the party claiming revision, always provided that such ignorance was not due to negligence.
2. The proceedings for revision shall be opened by a judgment of the Court expressly recording the existence of the new fact, recognizing that it has such a character as to lay the case open to revision, and declaring the application admissible on this ground.
3. The Court may require previous compliance with the terms of the judgment before it admits proceedings in revision.
4. The application for revision must be made at latest within six months of the discovery of the new fact.
5. No application for revision may be made after the lapse of ten years from the date of the judgment.

Article 62

1. Should a state consider that it has an interest of a legal nature which may be affected by the decision in the case, it may submit a request to the Court to be permitted to intervene.
2 It shall be for the Court to decide upon this request.

Article 63

1. Whenever the construction of a convention to which states other than those concerned in the case are parties is in question, the Registrar shall notify all such states forthwith.
2. Every state so notified has the right to intervene in the proceedings; but if it uses this right, the construction given by the judgment will be equally binding upon it.

Article 64

Unless otherwise decided by the Court, each party shall bear its own costs.

Chapter IV   Advisory Opinions

Article 65

1. The Court may give an advisory opinion on any legal question at the request of whatever body may be authorized by or in accordance with the Charter of the United Nations to make such a request.
2. Questions upon which the advisory opinion of the Court is asked shall be laid before the Court by means of a written request containing an exact statement of the question upon which an opinion is required, and accompanied by all documents likely to throw light upon the question.

Article 66

1. The Registrar shall forthwith give notice of the request for an advisory opinion to all states entitled to appear before the Court.
2. The Registrar shall also, by means of a special and direct communication, notify any state entitled to appear before the Court or international organization considered by the Court, or, should it not be sitting, by the President, as likely to be able to furnish information on the question, that the Court will be prepared to receive, within a time limit to be fixed by the President, written statements, or to hear, at a public sitting to be held for the purpose, oral statements relating to the question.
3. Should any such state entitled to appear before the Court have failed to receive the special communication referred to in paragraph 2 of this Article, such state may express a desire to submit a written statement or to be heard; and the Court will decide.
4. States and organizations having presented written or oral statements or both shall be permitted to comment on the statements made by other states or organizations in the form, to the extent,

and within the time limits which the Court, or, should it not be sitting, the President, shall decide in each particular case. Accordingly, the Registrar shall in due time communicate any such written statements to states and organizations having submitted similar statements.

Article 67

The Court shall deliver its advisory opinions in open court, notice having been given to the Secretary-General and to the representatives of Members of the United Nations, of other states and of international organizations immediately concerned.

Article 68

In the exercise of its advisory functions the Court shall further be guided by the provisions of the present Statute which apply in contentious cases to the extent to which it recognizes them to be applicable.

Chapter V   Amendment

Article 69

Amendments to the present Statute shall be effected by the same procedure as is provided by the Charter of the United Nations for amendments to that Charter, subject however to any provisions which the General Assembly upon recommendation of the Security Council may adopt concerning the participation of states which are parties to the present Statute but are not Members of the United Nations.

Article 70

The Court shall have power to propose such amendments to the present Statute as it may deem necessary, through written communications to the Secretary-General, for consideration in conformity with the provisions of Article 69.

Toward a Global Ethic

This interfaith declaration is the result of a two-year consultation among approximately two hundred scholars and theologians from many of the world's communities of faith. On September 2–4, 1993, the document was discussed by an assembly of religious and spiritual leaders meeting as part of the 1993 Parliament of the World's Religions in Chicago. Respected leaders from all the world's major faiths signed the *Declaration,* agreeing that it represents an initial effort — a point of beginning for a world sorely in need of ethical consensus. The Council for a Parliament of the World's Religions and those who have endorsed this text offer it to the world as an initial statement of the rules for living on which the world's religions agree.

The Declaration of a Global Ethic

The world is in agony. The agony is so pervasive and urgent that we are compelled to name its manifestations so that the depth of this pain may be made clear.

Peace eludes us . . . the planet is being destroyed . . . neighbors live in fear . . . women and men are estranged from each other . . . children die!

This is abhorrent!

We condemn the abuses of Earth's ecosystems.

We condemn the poverty that stifles life's potential; the hunger that weakens the human body; the economic disparities that threaten so many families with ruin.

We condemn the social disarray of the nations; the disregard for justice which pushes citizens to the margin; the anarchy overtaking our communities; and the insane death of children from violence. In particular we condemn aggression and hatred in the name of religion.

But this agony need not be.

It need not be because the basis for an ethic alreaady exists. This ethic offers the possibility of a better individual and global order, and leads individuals away from despair and societies away from chaos.

We are women and men who have embraced the precepts and practices of the world's religions.

We affirm that a common set of core values is found in the teachings of the religions, and that these form the basis of a global ethic.

We affirm that this truth is already known, but yet to be lived in heart and action.

We affirm that there is an errevocable, unconditional norm for all areas of life, for families and communities, for races, nations, and religions. There already exists ancient guidelines for human behavior which are found in the teachings of the religions of the world and which are the condition for a sustainable world order.

We Declare:

We are interdependent. Each of us depends on the well-being of the whole, and so we have respect for the community of living beings, for people, animals, and plants, and for the preservation of Earth, the air, water, and soil.

We take individual responsibility for all we do. All our decisions, actions, and failures to act have consequences.

We must treat others as we wish others to treat us. We make a commitment to respect life and dignity, individuality and diversity, so that every person is treated humanely, without exception. We must have patience and acceptance. We must be able to forgive, learning from the past but never allowing ourselves to be enslaved by memories of hate. Opening our hearts to one another, we must sink our narrow differences for the cause of the world community, practicing a culture of solidarity and relatedness.

We consider humankind our family. We must strive to be kind and generous. We must not live for ourselves alone, but should also serve others, never forgetting the children, the aged, the poor, the suffering, the disabled, the refugees, and the lonely. No person should ever be considered or treated as a second-class citizen, or be exploited in any way whatsoever. There should be equal partnership between men and women. We must not commit any kind of sexual immorality. We must put behind us all forms of domination or abuse.

We commit ourselves to a culture of nonviolence, respect, justice, and peace. We shall not oppress, injure, torture, or kill other human beings, forsaking violence as a means of settling differences.

We must strive for a just social and economic order, in which everyone has an equal chance to reach full potential as a human being. We must speak and act truthfully and with compassion, dealing fairly with all, and avoiding prejudice and hatred. We must not steal. We must move beyond the dominance of greed for power, prestige, money, and consumption to make a just and peaceful world.

Earth cannot be changed for the better unless the consciousness of individuals is changed first. We pledge to increase our awareness by disciplining our minds, by meditation, by prayer, or by positive thinking. Without risk and a readiness to sacrifice there can be no fundamental change in our situation. Therefore we commit ourselves to this global ethic, to understanding one another, and to socially beneficial, peace-fostering, and nature-friendly ways of life.

We invite all people, whether religious or not, to do the same.

Members of the Assembly who signed this Initial Declaration at the Parliament:

Tan Sri Dato' Seri Ahmad Sarji bin Abdul-Hamid (Muslim, Malaysia)
Prof. Masao Abe (Buddhist, Japan)
Dr. Thelma Adair (Christian, USA)
H.R.H. Oseijeman Adefunmi I (Indigenous, USA)
Dr. Hamid Ahmed (Muslim, India)
Mrs. Mazhar Ahmed (Muslim, India)

Pravrajka Amalaprana (Hindu, India)
Dastoor Dr. Kersey Antia (Zoroastrian, USA)
Mme. Nana Apeadu (Indigenous, Ghana)
Dr. M. Aram (Hindu, India)
Rev. Wesley Ariarajah (Christian, Switzerland)
Dr. A. T. Ariyaratne (Buddhist, Sri Lanka)
Imam Dawud Assud (Muslim, USA)
Jayashree Atavale Talwarkar (Hindu, India)
H.H. Shri Atmanandji (Jain, India)
H.I.G. Bambi Baaba (Indigenous, Uganda)
Rev. Thomas A Baima (Christian, USA)
Dr. Gerald O. Barney (Christian, USA)
H. Em. Joseph Cardinal Bernardin (Christian, USA)
Mr. Karl Berolzheimer (Jewish, USA)
Pere Pierre-François de Béthune (Christian, Belgium)
Dr. Nelvia M. Brady (Christian, USA)
Rev. Marcus Braybrooke (Christian, UK)
Dr. David Breed (Christian, USA)
Rabbi Herbert Bronstein (Jewish, USA)
Rev. John Buchanan (Christian, USA)
Mrs. Radha Burnier (Theosophist, India)
Rev. Baroness Cara-Marguerite-Drusilla, L.P.H. (Neo-Pagan, USA)
Mr. Blouke Carus (Christian, USA)
Mr. Peter V. Catches (Native American, USA)
Sister Joan M. Chatfield, M.M. (Christian, USA)
H.H. Swami Chidananda Saraswati (Hindu, India)
Swami Chidananda Saraswati Muniji (Hindu, USA)
Ms. Juana Conrad (Baha'i, USA)
H.H. The Dalai Lama (Buddhist, India)
Swami Dayananda Saraswati (Hindu, USA)
Counsellor Jacqueline Delahunt (Baha'i, USA)
Dr. Yvonee Delk (Christian, USA)
Sister Pratima Desai (Brahma Kumaris, USA)
Dr. Homi Dhalla (Zoroastrian, India)
Very Rev. R. Sheldon Duecker (Christian, USA)
Prof. Diana L. Eck (Christian, USA)
Dr. Wilma Ellis (Baha'i, USA)
Hon. Louis Farrakhan (Mulsim, USA)
Dr. Leon D. Finney, Jr. (Christian, USA)
Rev. Dr. James A. Forbes, Jr. (Christian, USA)
Dr. Rashmikani Gardi (Jain, USA)
Mr. Dipchand S. Gardi (Jain, USA)
Mrs. Maria Svolos Gebhard (Christian, USA)
Preah Maha Ghosananda (Buddhist, Cambodia)
Dr. Daniel Gómez-Ibáñez (Interfaith, USA)
Dr. Hamid Abdul Hai (Muslim, USA)

Dr. Mohammed Hamidulla (Muslim, Uganda)
B.K. Jagdish Chander Hassija (Brahma Kumaris, India)
Rev. Theodore M. Hesburgh, C.S.C. (Christian, USA)
Prof. Susanna Heschel (Jewish, USA)
Dr. Aziza al Hibri (Muslim, USA)
Mr. Chungliang Al Huang (Taoist, USA)
Dr. Asad Husain (Muslim, USA)
Dato Dr. Haji Ismail bin Ibrahim (Muslim, USA)
Prof. Ephraim Isaac (Jewish, USA)
Hon. Narendra P. Jain (Jain, India)
Dastoor Dr. Kaikhusroo Minocher JamaspAsa (Zoroastrian, India)
Very Rev. Frederick C. James (Christian, USA)
Ma Jaya Bhagavati (Interfaith, USA)
Ajahn Phra Maha Surasak Jvnando (Buddhist, USA)
Dr. Chatswmarn Kabilsingh (Buddhist, Thailand)
Abbot Timothy Kelly OSB (Christian, USA)
Mr. Jim Kenney (Christian, USA)
Sadguru Sant Keshavadas (Hindu, India)
Siri Singh Sahib Bhai Sahib Harbhajan Singh Khalsa Yogiji (Sikh, USA)
Dr. Irfan Ahmad Khan (Muslim, USA)
Dr. Qadir Husain Khan (Muslim, India)
Mr. P. V. Krishnayya (Hindu, USA)
Dr. Lakshmi Kumari (Hindu, India)
Prof. Dr. Hans Küng (Christian, Germany)
Mr. Peter Lawrence (Jewish, USA)
Ms. Dolores Leakey (Christian, USA)
Rev. Chung Ok Lee (Buddhist, USA)
Mrs. Norma U. Levitt (Jewish, USA)
Rev. Deborah Ann Light (Neo-Pagan, USA)
Mr. Amrish Mahajan (Hindu, USA)
Sister Joan Monica McGuire, O.P. (Christian, USA)
Imam Warith Deen Mohammed (Muslim, USA)
Very Rev. James Parks Morton (Christian, USA)
Mr. Archie Mosay (Native American, USA)
Dr. Robert Muller (Christian, Costa Rica)
Rev. Albert Nambiaparambil, CMI (Christian, India)
Prof. Seyyed Hossein Nasr (Muslim, USA)
Prof. James Nelson (Christian, USA)
Mr. Charles Nolley (Baha'i, USA)
Rev. Koshin Ogui, Sensei (Buddhist, USA)
Dastoor Jehangir Oshidari (Zoroastrian, Iran)
Dr. Abdel Rahman Osman (Muslim, USA)
Luang Poh Panyananda (Buddhist, Thailand)
Ven. Achahn Dr. Chuen Phangcham (Buddhist, USA)
Pravrajika Praabuddhaprana (Hindu, India)
B.K. Dadi Prakashmani (Brahma Kumaris, India)

Mr. Burton Pretty On Top (Native American, USA)
Rev. Dr. David Ramage, Jr. (Christian, USA)
Ven. Dr. Havanpola Ratanasara (Buddhist, USA)
Dr. Krishna Reddy (Hindu, USA)
Prof. V. Madhusudan Reddy (Hindu, India)
Mrs. Robert Reneker (Christian, USA)
Rev. Dr. Syngum Rhee (Christian, USA)
Mr. Rohinton Rivema (Zoroastrian, USA)
Lady Olivia Robertson (Neo-Pagan, Eire)
Most Rev. Placido Rodriguez (Christian, USA)
Most Rev. Willy Romelus (Christian, Haiti)
Ven. Seung Sahn (Buddhist, USA)
Swami Satchidananda (Hindu, USA)
Ms. Dorothy Savage (Christian, USA)
Rabbi Herman Schaalman (Jewish, USA)
Hon. Syed Shahabuddin (Muslim, India)
Bhai Mohinder Singh (Sikh, USA)
Dr. Karan Singh (Hindu, India)
Dr. Mehervan Singh (Sikh, Singapore)
Mr. Hardial Singh (Sikh, India)
Mr. Indarjit Singh (Sikh, UK)
Singh Sahib Jathedar Manjit Singh (Sikh, India)
Dr. Balwani Singh Hansra (Sikh, USA)
H.E. Dr. L. M. Singhvi (Jain, UK)
Ms. R. Leilani Smith (Baha'i, USA)
Ms. Helen Spector (Jewish, USA)
Brother David Steindl-Rast, OSB (Christian, USA)
H.H. Satguru Sivaya Subramuniyaswami (Hindu, USA)
Dr. Howard A. Sulkin (Jewish, USA)
Ven. Samu Surim (Buddhist, USA)
Hon. Homi Taleyarkhan (Zoroastrian, India)
Mr. John B. Taylor (Christian, Switzerland)
Brother Wayne Teasdale (Christian, USA)
Rev. Robert Traer (Unitarian, UK)
Dr. William F. Vendley (Christian, USA)
Pravrajika Vivekaprana (Hindu, India)
Prof. Henry Wilson (Christian, Switzerland)
Ven. Dr. Mapalagama Wipulasara Maha Thero (Buddhist, Sri Lanka)
Ms. Yael Wurmfeld (Baha'i, USA)
Rev. Addie Wyatt (Christian, USA)
H.H. Dr. Bala Siva Yogindra Maharaj (Hindu, India)
Baba Metahochi Kofi Zannu (Indigenous, Nigeria)
Dastoor Kobad Zarolia (Zoroastrian, Canada)
Dastoor Mehraban Zarthosty (Zoroastrian, Canada)